Leasehold disput(

a guide to Leasehold Valuation Tribunals

Francis Davey is a barrister. He became interested in Leasehold Valuation Tribunals when supplying free legal representation before tribunals while at the College of Law. Francis was involved in reforming the LVTs' procedures to deal with their new jurisdictions under the Commonhold and Leasehold Reform Act 2002. He gives advice sessions for leaseholders at Islington Law Centre and speaks to leaseholder groups on their rights.

Justin Bates is a barrister at Arden Chambers, specialising in all aspects of residential property and housing law. He previously acted as a pro bono adviser for the College of Law Tribunal Advice Service. He was formerly an editor of the *University of Toronto Law Review* and a founding editor of the *University of Toronto Journal of Law and Equality*. Justin also writes for the *European Human Rights Reports*.

The Legal Action Group is a national, independent charity which campaigns for equal access to justice for all members of society. Legal Action Group:
- provides support to the practice of lawyers and advisers
- inspires developments in that practice
- campaigns for improvements in the law and the administration of justice
- stimulates debate on how services should be delivered.

Leasehold disputes

a guide to Leasehold Valuation Tribunals

Francis Davey and Justin Bates

Legal Action Group
2004

This edition published in Great Britain 2004
by LAG Education and Service Trust Limited
242 Pentonville Road, London N1 9UN
www.lag.org.uk

British Library Cataloguing in Publication Data
a CIP catalogue record for this book is available from the British Library.

Crown copyright material is produced with the permission of the Controller of HMSO and the Queen's Printer for Scotland.

ISBN-10 1 903307 27 9
ISBN-13 978 1 903307 27 9

Typeset by Regent Typesetting, London
Printed in Great Britain by Bell & Bain Limited, Glasgow

Francis: For Helen Snape, who kept Justin and me supplied with food and drink while we worked on the book and who patiently read through all the text as we wrote it.

Justin: For my brother, Ryan, of whom I am always proud.

Preface

When we first began to give pro bono advice on Leasehold Valuation Tribunals (LVTs) it very quickly became clear that there was a considerable amount of relevant law, from a variety of sources, that had never been collected together. It is as a result of that experience that we have written this book.

LVTs are a development of Rent Assessment Panels, which have for many years assessed the fairness of rents. These panels were drafted in to carry out the valuations necessary in leasehold enfranchisement and, when they were making leasehold valuation decisions, they acquired the name 'Leasehold Valuation Tribunals'. Subsequently LVTs have gained a jurisdiction over service charges, and most recently a whole collection of new jurisdictions have been or will be added by the Commonhold and Leasehold Reform Act 2002.

There seems to be a clear policy of transferring questions, which require expert knowledge of residential property, to the LVT. The result of this is that the work of Rent Assessment Panels is now overshadowed by the much larger and growing work of the LVT.

This book is aimed at anyone likely to find themselves before or considering applying to an LVT. We hope it is comprehensive enough to satisfy the needs of lawyers and advisers who regularly work in the LVT, as well as being accessible enough for users to represent themselves at tribunal hearings.

This book does not cover the subject of leasehold enfranchisement: the subject is well covered elsewhere and any tenants involved in an enfranchisement will almost certainly need to instruct solicitors since it is a form of property purchase. In addition we have only mentioned Estate Management Schemes in passing because they are very rarely encountered in practice. We hope to have covered all remaining areas of the LVT's jurisdiction.

This book is confined to the LVTs that operate in England. Separate regulations have been made for Wales, where the LVT is administered by the Welsh Assembly.

It is normal in the context of residential landlord and tenant law for the terms 'leaseholder' and 'tenant' to be used in opposition. The former referring to a tenant under a long lease, while the latter is used to refer to someone with a shorter interest. This distinction is not one made in the legislation, nor is it a useful one in the context of most of the LVT's jurisdiction which is not confined to long leaseholders. For this reason the term 'tenant' will be used throughout this book inclusively.

In the legislation the term 'landlord' usually, but not exclusively, refers not only to the lessor, but also to anyone with a right to collect service charges. Unless the context suggests otherwise we have chosen to use the latter definition throughout.

The law is stated as at 6 April 2004. Where possible, reference has been made to more recent law at proof stage. The authors welcome any corrections, suggestions or other correspondence, which should be directed to the publisher.

Francis Davey
Gray's Inn

Justin Bates
Arden Chambers

July 2004

Contents

APPENDICES

Table of cases

Table of statutes

Table of statutory instruments

Abbreviations

CLRA 2002	Commonhold and Leasehold Reform Act 2002
CO2	Commonhold and Leasehold Reform Act 2002 (Commencement No 2 and Savings) (England) Order 2003 SI No 1986
Consultation Regs 2003	Service Charges (Consultation Requirements) (England) Regulations 2003
EMS	Estate management scheme
Fees Regs	Leasehold Valuation Tribunals (Fees) (England) Regulations 2003
LA 1980	Limitation Act 1980
LRHUDA 1993	Leasehold Reform, Housing and Urban Development Act 1993
LTA 1985	Landlord and Tenant Act 1985
LTA 1987	Landlord and Tenant Act 1987
LVT Regs 2003	Leasehold Valuation Tribunals (Procedure) (England) Regulations 2003
LVT	Leasehold Valuation Tribunal
PTR	Pre-trial review
QLTA	Qualifying long-term agreement
RAC	Rent Assessment Committee
RAP	Rent Assessment Panel
RICS	Royal Institute of Chartered Surveyors
RPTS	Residential Property Tribunal Service
RTA	Recognised tenants' association
RTB	Right to Buy tenancy
RTM	Right to Manage
SCO 1988	Service Charge (Estimates and Consultation) Order 1988
TMO	Tenant management organisation

Introduction

1.1   This book is intended to give advice for residential tenants in a dispute with their landlords which might bring them before a Leasehold Valuation Tribunal.

History

1.2   Leasehold Valuation Tribunals are another name for Rent Assessment Committees. Rent Assessment Committees (RACs) were set up to adjudicate disputes concerning the registration of rents under the Rent Acts. RACs consist of three people: a legally qualified 'chair' and two 'wing members' who will not normally be lawyers but are appointed because of their expertise in housing.

1.3   The Housing Act 1980 transferred jurisdiction over leasehold enfranchisement to RACs. While exercising this jurisdiction an RAC is called a Leasehold Valuation Tribunal (LVT). An LVT is therefore an RAC which is exercising certain powers given to it. When sitting as an LVT an RAC is governed by different procedural rules, and at least one member must 'be experienced in the valuation of land'.

1.4   The Landlord and Tenant Act (LTA) 1985 gave LVTs the power to determine whether any service charge paid by the tenant of a flat (later a dwelling) was reasonable. This proved to be a fertile source of applications to the LVT, so much so that it has eclipsed much of its other work.

1.5   The LTA 1987 created a power of the LVT to appoint a manager to manage residential leasehold property, where the existing management had been defective for some reason. The LVT could supervise the appointed manager, vary the manager's remit or dismiss them. Tenants were also given the right to challenge their landlord's choice of insurer before the LVT.

1.6   Over the years it became clear that there were a number of problems with the LVT's jurisdiction.

1.7   Tenants had experienced considerable frustration with the narrowness of the LVTs' power to decide questions concerning service charges. All the LVT was empowered to do was rule on whether a charge was reasonable; it was given no power to decide whether the charge was properly payable on construction of the lease; or whether statutory consultation requirements had been complied with. Tenants were forced to frame many applications so that they appeared to be reasonableness challenges, hiding a challenge that was really being brought on some other ground.

1.8   The LVT did not have jurisdiction over 'improvements', which

were not part of the statutory definition of a service charge.[1] Much
time was spent in arguing whether work done by a landlord was an
'improvement' or a 'repair', a distinction which was hard to make in
any principled way in practice.

1.9   In 2001 the problems faced by tenants were further compounded
by the decision of the Court of Appeal in *R v London Leasehold Valuation Tribunal ex p Daejan Properties Ltd*[2] which ruled that, where a
tenant had already paid a service charge, they would not normally be
able to challenge the charge before an LVT, drastically reducing the
scope of the LVT's power.

1.10   The Commonhold and Leasehold Reform Act (CLRA) 2002
addressed many of these problems and extended the LVT's power to
consider any question concerning the payability of a service charge;
the definition of service charges was enlarged to include 'improvements'; and it was expressly provided that a challenge could still be
made even where a tenant had already paid the charge.

1.11   The CLRA 2002 also created a new 'Right to Manage' (RTM). Prior
to the 2002 Act the LVT could appoint a new manager only if some
defect were shown in the existing management arrangements. RTM
allows tenants to set up a company, known as an RTM company. If a
majority of tenants join the company and go through the correct procedure, the landlord can be forced to accept the RTM company as a
new manager, regardless of whether there is any fault in the existing
management.

1.12   Service charge litigation revealed that there were a number of
charges being levied by landlords that did not fall into the statutory
definition of a service charge, but which might still be unreasonable
and constitute a burden on the tenant. The most common such
charges are now known as 'administration charges', and the LVT is
given a very similar jurisdiction over them as it has for service charges.

1.13   An existing power, possessed by the court, to vary inadequate
leases has been extended to the LVT, and the power to create a new set
of procedural rules for the LVT was introduced.

Organisation

1.14   LVTs are administered in England by the Residential Property Tribunal Service (RPTS), which is a part of the Office of the Deputy

1   LTA 1985 s18.
2   (2001) 3 EGLR 28.

Prime Minister. In Wales the LVT is the responsibility of the Welsh Assembly. The Welsh LVT is governed by very similar rules to that in England, but will not be dealt with in this book.[3]

1.15   England is divided into a number of regional Rent Assessment Panels, from which the members of the LVT are drawn. Chairs are appointed by the Lord Chancellor, other members being appointed by the Deputy Prime Minister. Appointment is to a specific panel, though some members are members of more than one panel. Almost all Panel members work part-time, the principal exception being the Senior President, who is also the president of the London panel and is assisted by three full-time Vice-Presidents.

Hearings

1.16   Hearings can take place anywhere, and are often held in public build-ings, such as civic centres or church halls, hired for the purpose. It is even possible for an LVT to meet in the property itself, for example, in the case of a disabled tenant who would find it otherwise very difficult to attend the tribunal elsewhere. Some of the Panels, in particular the London Panel, have dedicated hearing rooms, and when they are available, hearings will usually take place there.

1.17   The intention is that hearings should avoid the formality of a courtroom so that they are not intimidating for lay applicants. All par-ticipants remain seated throughout a hearing and no court dress is used. An LVT is free to decide on the procedure it adopts at a hearing, which gives a great deal of flexibility which should be used to put lay applicants further at their ease.

1.18   Despite these measures, many disputes in front of an LVT can become factually or legally complex. Applicants often find it difficult to organise their cases clearly and to appreciate points of law raised against them. This can only become more of a problem as LVTs gain a more complex set of jurisdictions.

1.19   Applicants are free to represent themselves or to appoint any other representative (who need not be legally qualified) to speak for them. There are valuers and surveyors who make a practice of appearing before LVTs (mostly on behalf of landlords).

1.20   No public funding is available for representation at an LVT and it can be difficult and expensive for tenants to obtain representation. The LEASE advice service provides a telephone advice line and help-

---

3   SI 2004 No 681.

ful introductory publications concerning LVTs.[4] In London, the College of Law offers a free advice and representation service, which is staffed by student lawyers.[5]

Precedent

1.21 LVTs are not courts, and their decisions are not binding on one another. LVTs behave as if they were bound by decisions of the High Court, the Lands Tribunal and all higher courts. Appeals from a decision of the LVT may be made, with permission of the either Tribunal, to the Lands Tribunal, and from there to the Court of Appeal.

1.22 Past decisions of LVTs, dating back to 1998, can be found at the LEASE website.[6] It is envisaged that the RPTS will provide a similar service at some stage in the future.

Outline of this book

1.23 Chapter 2 deals with what is currently the most important area of the LVT's jurisdiction, service charges. It discusses the existing case law on their payability and discusses changes made by the CLRA 2002. In considering whether and how to challenge a service charge demand, it is important for a tenant to have as much information as possible. Chapter 3 explains what rights a tenant has to demand information from or have information supplied by their landlord.

1.24 When landlords undertake large works, or enter into contracts lasting longer than a year, to which their tenants will have to contribute in their service charges, they are required to go through a relatively elaborate consultation process concerning their work. Should they fail to consult properly the amount they are allowed to recover from their tenants is capped. The law on consultation is covered in chapter 4.

1.25 Sometimes a tenant is required to pay insurance to an insurer that has been chosen by a landlord. Such payments are not service charges, so that a tenant would not be able to challenge them in the normal way. An LVT has a jurisdiction to hear a challenge by a tenant to such insurance arrangements; this is the subject of chapter 5.

---

4   See www.lease-advice.org.
5   See appendix A for contact details.
6   www.lease-advice.org.

1.26   Chapter 6 deals with certain miscellaneous charges, called administration charges, that might be recovered by a landlord from a tenant and that are not covered by the definition of service charges. The power of an LVT over administration charges is similar to, but not quite the same as, that which it exercises over service charges.

1.27   Sometimes the root of a dispute between landlord and tenant is a poorly drafted lease. Any party to a lease can apply to an LVT to have the lease altered (varied) on various grounds. Chapter 7 explores the situations when such a variation can be ordered, and the process by which variation takes place.

1.28   Chapter 8, describes the power of an LVT to appoint a manager where there has been some failure of management of a property; and also the ways in which LVTs supervise a manager once appointed. Chapter 9 discusses the alternative route by which tenants may force the appointment of their own management company, a so-called RTM company, regardless of any preceding fault.

1.29   Chapter 10 gives a very brief sketch of the power that a landlord has to take back the property they have leased if the tenant is at fault in paying the rent or complying with a covenant in their lease. This is a process known as forfeiture and would be quite severe. However, for residential leases the law has curbed the power of landlords to forfeit in various ways. Chapter 10 explains how the LVT becomes involved in a forfeiture situation.

1.30   Tenants involved in the purchase of their freehold, or an extension or renewal of their lease should expect to have legal advice (since they are involved in a process of conveyancing). This book does not attempt to deal with the LVT's jurisdiction over leasehold enfranchisement, which will be largely ignored hereafter.

CHAPTER 2

Service charges

continued

Key points

- A service charge is any variable sum of money paid by the tenant which is payable, directly or indirectly, for services, repairs, maintenance, improvements, insurance or management of the property. It may or may not be included in the tenant's rent.
- A landlord may not recover for something that is not clearly set out in the lease. Courts interpret alleged service charge clauses restrictively.
- Service charges relate to services actually provided. They are not a source of profit for landlords.
- As a general rule, the fact that a tenant is behind with service charge payments does not allow a landlord to stop providing services.
- The LVT may decide whether a service charge is payable.
- An LVT may also decide the person to whom service charges are payable; who is liable to pay the charge; the amount which is payable; the date and the manner of payment.
- The fact that a tenant has paid a service charge does not prevent an application to the LVT.
- Anyone may apply to an LVT for a determination of the payability of a service charge. Most applications are made by either tenants, landlords or managing agents.
- All service charges must be demanded within 18 months of being incurred.
- Landlords who arrange insurance for a property and recover the cost as a service charge must reduce the charge to their tenants by the amount of any commission they receive.
- Landlords hold service charge contributions on trust.

Tips for advisers

- The argument 'if the landlord had acted sooner the work now charged for would have been less extensive and expensive' is a commonly heard complaint. It is possible to run this argument in an LVT, but evidence is often a practical difficulty.
- There is a wealth of case law on the distinction between repairs and improvements. The distinction has less importance after the Commonhold and Leasehold Reform Act 2002 reforms.
- It is unclear whether the principle of set-off applies in the LVT.
- There is probably no limitation period for a tenant to bring a service charge dispute before the LVT.

Introduction

2.1   Service charges are one of the most common areas of dispute between tenants and landlords[1] to come before LVTs and such disputes comprise the majority of its workload. The most common disputes concern:

a) whether the service charge needs to be incurred;
b) whether the service charge represents value for money;
c) whether the service charge is being apportioned fairly;
d) whether the work in respect of which the service charge is levied is a repair or an improvement;
e) the operation of a reserve fund;
f) whether any set-off can be taken into account when calculating service charges.

2.2   All these points will be dealt with in this chapter. Landlords are usually obliged to consult tenants before undertaking major works. Disputes about whether or not consultation has been properly carried out are frequent and the subject of consultation will be dealt with separately in chapter 4.

2.3   Many leases allow the landlord to recover the cost of insuring the property from tenants. Where these costs are recovered as service charges, they may be challenged as such. Specific points that arise in respect of insurance are dealt with at para 2.41 below.

What is a service charge?

2.4   A service charge is an amount payable by the tenant of a dwelling as part of or in addition to the rent:

(i) which is payable, directly or indirectly, for services, repairs, maintenance, improvements or insurance or the landlord's costs of management; and
(ii) the whole or part of which varies or may vary according to the relevant costs.[2]

What is not a service charge

2.5   Some charges, such as those for giving consent to alterations, may be administration charges (see chapter 6). Where a lease sets a fixed

---

1   Meaning, for this purpose, anyone with the right to enforce payment of service charges. See Landlord and Tenant Act (LTA) 1985 s30.
2   LTA 1985 s18(1)(a).

charge for a service, that charge is not a 'service charge' within the meaning of the Landlord and Tenant Act 1985. Where such provisions are unsatisfactory, it may be possible to apply to an LVT for the variation of the offending term of the lease (see chapter 7). The inclusion of 'improvements' in the definition of 'service charge' was added by the Commonhold and Leasehold Reform Act (CLRA) 2002, with effect from 30 September 2003. It does not apply to service charges incurred before that date.[3]

General rules about service charges

2.6   There are some general rules about service charges:

a) Service charge clauses are to be read restrictively and only permit recovery for items clearly included in the clause.[4] This means that, among other things, interest on service charges is not recoverable without clear words to that effect.

b) Service charge clauses may allow for the recovery of capital as well as running costs, although this must be made clear in the lease.[5]

c) Service charges should only allow the landlord to recoup the costs of services supplied. They are not an additional source of profit.

d) A service charge clause cannot impose on the tenant liability to pay for matters falling within the landlord's implied repairing obligations under Landlord and Tenant Act (LTA) 1985 s11 and is void to the extent that it purports to do so.[6]

e) In the absence of clear words to the contrary, the obligation on the landlord to provide services is independent of the tenant's duty to pay for them. This means that arrears of service charges will not entitle a landlord to cease providing services.[7]

'Sweeping up' clauses

2.7   In recent years landlords have attempted to include a clause or clauses in the lease, the aim of which is to allow them to recover all

---

3   Commonhold and Leasehold Reform Act 2002 (Commencement No 2 and Savings) (England) Order 2003 SI No 1986, Sch 2 para 2.

4   *Gilje v Charlgrove Securities* [2002] L&TR, 33; [2002] 1 EGLR 41 per Mummery LJ.

5   *Lloyds Bank v Bowker Orford* [1992] 2 EGLR 44; *Yorkbrook Investments v Batten* [1985] 2 EGLR 100

6   LTA 1985 s11.

7   See *Yorkbrook Investments v Batten* [1985] 2 EGLR 100; *Gordon v Selico Co* [1986] 1 EGLR 71.

expenditure not already covered by another clause in the lease. These are known as 'sweeping up' clauses.

2.8   When such clauses have been considered by the courts they have been construed restrictively. Landlords will not be able to recover any expenditure that is not clearly intended in the lease, as the following examples will illustrate.

Example 1

A lease contained a provision which allowed recovery of repairs and a proviso that the landlord might, at their reasonable discretion, hold, add to, extend, vary or make any alteration in the rendering of the services at any time in their absolute discretion, provided that it would make for more efficient management and conduct of the building.

This did not cover repairs to external walls where this was not already expressly included. The wide words were to be read as only relating to works for which he could already charge, not as a discretionary powers to add more works to that list.[8]

Example 2

A provision entitling a landlord to recover the cost of providing and maintaining additional services or amenities did not permit the landlord to recover the cost of installing double glazed windows.[9]

Example 3

A clause allowed the maintenance trustee to recover costs associated with works necessary to maintain the building as a high class block of flats. This would go beyond repair but did not extend to the maintainance of the structure of the building, but covered things such as high speed lifts and air conditioning which would be unique to a high class block of flats.[10]

Example 4

'The cost of all other services which the lessor may, at its absolute discretion, provide or install . . .' did not cover legal fees relating to an action against the tenants.[11]

---

8   *Jacob Isbicki v Goulding* [1989] 1 EGLR 236.
9   *Mullaney v Maybourne* [1986] 1 EGLR 70.
10   *Holding and Management v Property Holding* [1989] 1 WLR 1313.
11   *St Mary's Mansions v Limegate Investment* [2002] EWCA Civ 1491; [2002] 43 EG 161.

Grounds for applying to the Leasehold Valuation Tribunal

2.9 Before 30 September 2003, LVTs were only able to decide whether a service charge was or was not reasonable.[12] The CLRA 2002 made a radical change; an LVT now decides what is payable.[13] Of course a service charge is only payable in so far as it is reasonable, and so reasonableness is still an important concept but it is no longer the only one.

2.10 In addition to deciding whether or not a service charge is payable, an LVT may also decide:[14]

- the person by whom it is payable;
- the person to whom it is payable;
- the amount which is payable;
- the date at or by which it is payable; and
- the manner in which it is payable.

2.11 It is immaterial whether or not the tenant has paid the service charge in dispute.[15] It is also not to be presumed that, merely because a tenant has paid the disputed service charges, he or she has agreed or admitted any matter.[16]

2.12 An LVT may not hear an application concerning a service charge which:[17]

- has been agreed or admitted by the tenant;
- has been, or is to be, referred to arbitration pursuant to a post-dispute arbitration agreement to which the tenant is a party;
- has been the subject of determination by a court; or
- has been the subject of determination by an arbitral tribunal pursuant to a post-dispute arbitration agreement.

2.13 An LVT is neither a court, nor an arbitral tribunal, and so there is no reason in principle why an LVT may not hear an application concerning service charges that have been the subject of a previous determination by the LVT. For example, where a determination was based on

---

12 For the old law see the former LTA 1985 s19(2A) and (2B).

13 CLRA 2002 s27A.

14 LTA 1985 s27A(1).

15 LTA 1985 s27A(2). Overturning the decision *R (Daejan Properties Ltd) v London Leasehold Valuation Tribunal* [2001] EWCA Civ 1095 on this point.

16 LTA 1985 s27A(5).

17 LTA 1985 s27A(4).

an optimistic set of estimates generated by a landlord, that were revised upwards once work had been tendered.[18]

2.14   Such an application would be subject to the power of the LVT to strike out applications for being an abuse of process (see below, para 11.50).

Would a service charge be payable?

2.15   LVTs also have prospective powers. An LVT may determine whether, if costs were incurred for services, repairs, maintenance, improvements, insurance or management of any specified description, a service charge would be payable for the costs and, if it would, an LVT may determine:[19]

(a) the person by whom it would be payable,
(b) the person to whom it would be payable,
(c) the amount which would be payable,
(d) the date at or by which it would be payable, and
(e) the manner in which it would be payable.

It is likely that this prospective power will present more difficulties for LVTs.

2.16   There should be little difficulty in determining, in advance, that, were work to be done by a landlord, the lease would allow them to recover costs for the work via service charges. For example, a landlord might wish to repair a boundary fence, but there could be a dispute with tenants about whether it was covered by terms of the lease. Either party could apply for a determination of this question, in advance, to the LVT. Such a determination would determine the payability of those charges if the work were done.

2.17   In a similar fashion, (a), (b), (d) and (e) above ask questions that are likely to be unproblematic. The difficulty comes with (c): the amount which would be payable. In the example above, once it has been determined that the cost of repairing the fence is recoverable under the lease, paragraph (c) would appear to allow an LVT to set a price for the work in advance. However, if the work, through no fault of the parties, was more expensive than had been predicted due to unforeseen difficulties; or if it were cheaper than had been expected; then the new price would surely be reasonable and hence payable.

2.18   There does not appear to be any principle that prevents either

18   *Re Compton Court, London SE19* LVTP/SC/008/091.
19   LTA 1985 s27A(3).

party to such a determination returning to the LVT for a new determination as to the reasonableness of the new sums. A recent LVT has
just done this.[20]

Completing the application form

2.19   It is quite often the case that work is due to be done when an application is first made to the LVT Service, but that by the time it is heard,
the work has been completed. For this reason, the application form
has been designed so that an application does not have to specify
whether they are applying under LTA 1985 s27A(1) (determination
that a service charge is payable) or section 27A(3) (determination that
if costs were incurred, a service charge would be payable for the
costs). All that an applicant needs to do is to indicate what it is they
want an LVT to determine and in respect of which service charge
years.

Which tenancies are affected?

2.20   The right to apply for a determination of the payability of service
charges, described in this chapter, applies only to residential tenancies. The only local authority tenancies to which this chapter applies
are those held by long leaseholders.[21] There is no reason why secure
tenants of Housing Associations should not be covered.

2.21   In practice, tenancies under short leases – those of less than seven
years[22] – are unlikely to be paying service charges because in such
leases the landlord is given the responsibility for the majority of
repair and maintenance.[23]

2.22   Statutory tenants and subtenants[24] are included. If rent has been
registered under the provisions of Rent Act 1977 Part IV, an application may only be made to an LVT in respect of service charges that
have been registered as variable.[25]

---

20 *Compton Court, Victoria Crescent, London SE19* LVTP/SC/008/091 and 092/01.
21 LTA 1985 s26.
22 LTA 1985 s13.
23 LTA 1985 s11.
24 LTA 1985 s30.
25 LTA 1985 s27.

Who may apply to an LVT?

2.23   There is no restriction on who may apply to an LVT for the determination of service charges. In practice most, if not all applications will be made by tenants, landlords and managing agents. There may be situations where some other party has an interest in a determination such as a guarantor of the service charges of a tenant.

2.24   Where an applicant has no financial interest in the outcome of a determination, they are likely to have their application struck out by the LVT as being frivolous (see para 11.50).

Issues for determination

Payability

2.25   As mentioned above at paragraph 2.6, when considering the question of whether a service charge is payable at all, it is normal practice for service charge provisions to be construed restrictively. Recovery in respect of items which are not clearly included is unlikely to be allowed.

2.26   However, courts have, at times, had to deal with ineptly drafted service charge clauses. In these situations, in an attempt to do justice between the parties, a more expansive approach has been taken. For example, in one case, a clause which, read literally, did not require a tenant to contribute fairly to the costs of maintaining the common areas, was construed in accordance with the obvious intentions of the parties to oblige the tenant to contribute towards such costs.[26]

2.27   A clause which requires a landlord to obtain and submit documents (for example estimates of the cost of work) as a condition on the recovery of the costs of such work, must be followed. If not, the landlord risks not being able to recover the costs involved.[27] This is in addition to any statutory obligations as to the supply of information to tenants (see chapter 3) or consultation (see chapter 4).

2.28   There are no reported decisions of an LVT dealing with the question of to whom a service charge was payable. If such a question were to arise it would most likely be approached as a question of interpretation of the lease.

26   *Billson v Tristrem* [2000] L&TR 220.
27   See *CIN Properties v Barclays Bank Plc* [1986] 1 EGLR 59 by way of example.

Reasonableness

2.29 Whether or not service charges are required to be reasonable at common law is unclear.[28] For the residential leases that are covered by this chapter, the common law position is irrelevant because LTA 1985 s19 makes it a statutory provision that service charges must be reasonable for them to be payable. Under LTA 1985 s19 reasonableness enters into the question of payability in two different ways. Service charges are only payable to the extent that they are reasonably incurred; and where they are incurred, only where the services or works for which they are incurred are of a reasonable standard.

2.30 For example, if a landlord replaces a roof and wishes to pass on the costs of replacement to the tenants, the tenants could complain that the replacement of the roof was unnecessary, in which case the costs would not be reasonably incurred. Alternatively, the new roof might be inadequate, in which case the tenants' challenge would be on the ground that the work was not done to a reasonable standard. The standard of work can be unreasonably high, as well as unreasonably low.

2.31 A challenge under either limb of LTA 1985 s19 may prevent the landlord recovering the whole of their costs.

2.32 The usual effect of a finding that costs were unreasonably incurred is that the costs are disallowed in their entirety. Where costs would have been reasonable, but the work or service was done to an unreasonably high standard, an LVT will usually find that a proportion of the costs were recoverable.

2.33 Where work has been done to an unreasonably low standard the approach of an LVT is likely to depend on the effect of the work that has been done. Some work of an unreasonably low standard may still have a useful and quantifiable value.

Burden of proof

2.34 On the question of the reasonableness of a service charge, there is no presumption either way.[29] In so far as the position has been analysed by the Court of Appeal, it would appear that where a tenant has challenged service charges as being unreasonable, and set out a clear case as to which items are disputed, the tenant need only put sufficient

---

28 Nicholas Roberts 'Service Charges, Daejan and Claims in Restitution' Conv 2003, Sep/Oct, 380–397, *Finchbourne Ltd v Rodrigues* [1976] 3 All ER 581, *Havenridge Ltd v Boston Dyers Ltd* [1994] 2 EGLR 73, CA.

29 *Yorkbrook Investments Ltd v Batten* [1985] 2 EGLR 100, CA.

evidence before the court to show that the question of reasonableness is arguable. It is then for the landlord to meet the tenant's allegations with evidence of their own.[30] The LVT will then make a decision based on the evidence before it.

2.35 Most other questions of payability will depend on the construction of the lease and so will not involve the calling of any evidence. All that would be required of the LVT is to decide on the meaning of the lease, which is a question of law and not of evidence.

General principles of reasonableness

2.36 No definition of 'unreasonable' is found in the legislation, and in each case it will be a question of fact. However, the courts have established the following general principles:

- The fact that something is contemplated in the lease does not automatically make it reasonable to incur costs in respect of that item. The fact that a porter for a block of flats was contemplated in a lease did not mean that a full-time porter, as opposed to a part-time porter, was reasonable.[31]

- The fact that it is 'reasonable' to have a service provided does not automatically mean that the costs associated with it will be 'reasonably incurred.' While it may be reasonable to have a cleaner provided for a block of flats, that will not necessarily mean that the particular cleaner in question represents costs 'reasonably incurred'.[32]

- The requirement that costs be 'reasonably incurred' does not mean that the relevant expenditure must be the cheapest available. On the other hand, the landlord may not charge a figure that is grossly out of line with the market norm.[33]

- When examining the method of repair (or provision of services) chosen by the landlord, the level to be reimbursed by the tenant will be assessed with reference to whether the landlord would have chosen this method of repair (or provision of services), if he or she were to bear the costs.[34] It follows from this that the correct perspective when examining the question of reasonableness is that of

---

30 [1985] 2 EGLR 100.
31 *Veena SA v Cheong* [2003] 1 EGLR 175.
32 [2003] 1 EGLR 175.
33 *Forcelux v Sweetman* [2001] 2 EGLR 173.
34 *Hyde Housing Association v George Williams* LRX/53/1999 (Lands Tribunal).

the landlord. It is for this reason that it will, for example, usually be reasonable to employ commercial cleaners, rather than consider what tenants would expect to pay domestic cleaners they hired in respect of their own homes.[35] Similarly, the fact that tenants may suggest that they could, acting individually, provide services cheaper than those provided by the landlord, is irrelevant. Landlords are entitled to use qualified personnel.[36]

- The fact that the landlord has adopted an appropriate procedure for incurring the costs does not mean that the costs will be reasonably incurred if they are in excess of an appropriate market rate.[37]

- Where services are not provided to a reasonable standard, then a deduction on account of the deficiency may be made and it need not be the case that the whole of a relevant item be disallowed.[38] Only in very exceptional circumstances will a court apply the *de minimis* principle to a reduction that is claimed by tenants in respect of service charges. Courts recognise that even where small amounts are disputed the sums may have great significance for those involved.[39]

- The fact that tenants have a time-limited interest in the property is a material factor when considering 'reasonableness'.[40] A tenant with a three-year lease could not be required to pay for roof replacement works which would fulfil the landlord's repairing obligations over 20 years or more when such works were not necessary to fulfil the obligations over the shorter period of the tenant's lease.

Neglect

2.37   Where a landlord has neglected to carry out repairs or maintenance for some time, the eventual cost of repair may be increased because of the historic neglect. In such circumstances a landlord may not recover the additional cost caused by their failure to repair, either by way of a service charge or other means.[41]

---

35 *Re Churstown Mansions* LON/00AG/LSL/2003/0105 (LVT).
36 *Colney Hatch Court Ltd v Sen* LON/00AC/LSC/2003/0006 (LVT).
37 *Forcelux v Sweetman* [2001] 2 EGLR 173.
38 *Yorkbrook Investments v Batten* [1985] 2 EGLR 100, in the context of Housing Finance Act 1972 s91A, which had similar material provisions.
39 *Yorkbrook Investments v Batten* [1985] 2 EGLR 100.
40 *Scottish Mutual Assurance Plc v Jardine Public Relations* [1999] EGCS 43.
41 *Loria v Hammer* [1989] 2 EGLR 249.

2.38   Strictly speaking this is a rule of recoverability, rather than reasonableness, though it has been treated as such in later cases.[42] The
effect of a breach of covenant to repair by the landlord is further discussed with the doctrine of set-off at paragraph 2.63 below.

2.39   In practice this 'historic neglect' argument rarely succeeds,
because tenants fail to produce convincing evidence that quantifies
the increase in cost of repair work due to the past neglect, hence the
question of reasonableness or recoverability never arises because the
tenant has done no more than assert that neglect has taken place.

2.40   Advisers should stress the importance of collecting cogent evidence that quantifies the additional costs occasioned by the historic
neglect. It would appear that no LVT has, to date, reduced a service
charge due to historic neglect.

Insurance

2.41   The following situations are a common cause of confusion:

a) the landlord is required under the terms of the lease to insure the
property and is permitted to recover the cost of insurance from the
tenants; and

b) the tenants are required to insure but only with an insurer selected
by the landlord.

2.42   In case (a) the insurance premiums form part of the tenants' service
charges and may be challenged under LTA 1985 s27A. In case (b) the
premium payments are not service charges, the tenants' only
recourse being to challenge the landlord's choice of insurer, which is
discussed in chapter 5.

2.43   Case (b) can, at times, be hard to distinguish from case (a). This is
particularly the case when the landlord acts as an agent for the insurance company. The tenants will pay the landlord their share of the
insurance premiums, but these payments will not be service charges
and so fall outside the protection discussed in this chapter. The lease
should make it clear whether the obligation to insure is on the landlord or the tenant and thus whether any insurance costs are recovered
as service charges.

---

42   *Wandsworth LBC v Griffin* [2000] 26 EG 147; *Re Blocks 94–110, 123–139,
152–168 Claypond Gardens* LVT/SC/032//029/02, LVT/SCC/032//021/02.

Commissions

2.44 Landlords are often paid large commissions for selecting particular insurers who then recover the cost of the commission via higher premium payments which will ultimately be borne by the tenants. The landlord will, by an indirect route, be profiting from the tenants, something they are not entitled to do. In those circumstances the service charges can be challenged under LTA 1985 s27A for being unreasonable. When considering what is a reasonable sum to pay for insurance via a service charge, the starting point is the amount that the landlord would have incurred had they been obliged to pay for the insurance of the property themselves.

2.45 In practice this means that the landlord should not be able to recover more than the net of the amount of the insurance premium less any commission received.[43] A landlord may argue that they are entitled to some compensation for their administrative costs in arranging the insurance. Such a payment may only be recovered from tenants if there is a provision of the lease allowing such recovery, and would in any case have to be reasonable. The right to be provided with information concerning the insurance that the landlord has effected in order to facilitate such a challenge is discussed at para 5.39 below.

Improvements

Relevance

2.46 While many leases permit a landlord to recover as a service charge the cost of any repairs done to the property, most private leases did not allow a landlord to recover for work done to improve the property that went beyond a mere repair. This distinction was always a difficult one to make as any repair will at the same time improve a property to some extent. A helpful formulation of this point was suggested by HHJ Rich QC in *Gibson Investments Ltd v Chesterton Plc*:[44]

> ... a scheme of work either constitutes repair, and even though it involves betterment is not therefore an improvement, or it is an improvement.

2.47 In addition to its application to the construction of repairing covenants in a lease, the idea that 'repairs' and 'improvements' should be treated differently, was given relevance to the LVT's jurisdiction over

43 For example *Peile v Executors of WAC Maidman* LVT/SC/025/010/98.
44 [2003] EWHC 1255 (ChD).

service charges by LTA 1985 s18. This section restricted the definition of a service charge, and hence the LVT's jurisdiction, to 'services, repairs, maintenance or insurance or the landlord's costs of management'. This was taken by LVTs to exclude any jurisdiction over 'improvements'.

2.48   Section 18 does not refer to 'improvements'. The correct approach for an LVT would be to decide whether particular work fell within the definition of a 'repair', but in practice the approach adopted by most LVTs was to decide whether work was an 'improvement' and, if it was so found, to decline jurisdiction. If 'improvement' is simply used as a shorthand for 'an improvement that goes beyond a repair to the extent that it is no longer a repair' there is nothing objectionable in the latter approach, but it is far from clear that all LVTs were alive to this distinction.

2.49   The question of the LVT's proper approach to its jurisdiction in respect of improvements will increasingly be of historic interest as the jurisdiction of LVTs has been widened[45] over costs incurred on or after 30 September 2003[46] to expressly include improvements. The distinction remains relevant to the construction of service charge provisions in a lease. It will also continue to be of importance to any challenge to service charges for works of improvement where costs were incurred before 30 September 2003.

What is an improvement?[46a]

2.50   There is a considerable body of case law, in which the courts have emphasised that there is no single test to determine whether particular works are improvements or repairs. In practice it will be a question of fact and degree in each case. To the extent that any general principles can be gleaned from the authorities, the following would seem to be of some relevance.

2.51   In *McDougall v Easington*,[47] Mustill LJ canvassed a number of authorities and suggested three possible tests, 'which may be applied separately or concurrently as the circumstances of the individual case may demand':

i) whether the alterations went to the whole or substantially the whole of the structure or to only a subsidiary part;

---

45   CLRA 2002 Sch 9 para 7.
46   Commonhold and Leasehold Reform Act 2002 (Commencement No 2 and Savings) (England) Order 2003, Sch 2 para 2.
46a The authors are grateful to Ross Fentem for his research on this point.
47   58 P&CR 201; 21 HLR 310 at 316, CA.

ii) whether the effect of the alterations was to produce a building of a wholly different character from that which had been let;

iii) what was the cost of the works in relation to the previous value of the building, and what was their effect on the value and lifespan of the building?

Another formulation of this question is: 'is the repair so radical and extravagant as to amount to creating a new thing in place of what was there and not a mere replacement?'[48]

2.52   A useful example of the different outcomes that can be reached on superficially similar facts is provided by two cases on window-replacement: *Mullaney v Maybourne Grange (Croydon) Management Co Ltd*,[49] and *Minja Properties Ltd v Cussins Property Group plc*.[50]

2.53   In both cases, single-glazed windows were replaced with double-glazed ones. In *Mullaney*, the original windows were leaking water; in *Minja*, the original frames were rotten. However, the cost of installing double-glazing in *Mullaney* amounted to almost double the cost of installing windows similar to the orignal ones. This led Mr Jeffs QC to consider the work an improvement. By contrast, in *Minja*, Harman J reasoned that the cost of 'repairing' the rotten frames with frames that would take double-glazing was only trivially greater than installing frames to take single-glazing. So too, the subsequent installation of two panes of glass would only amount to a trivial increase in cost. Therefore, the proposed work amounted to a repair.

Apportionment

2.54   Service charges are only recoverable to the extent permitted under the lease, hence the apportionment between tenants is to be governed by the terms specified in the lease. Typically a lease will apportion service charges in one of four ways:

1) by floor area;
2) by rateable value;
3) by fixed proportions; or
4) by a duty to pay a 'fair proportion' or words to that effect.

Apportionment by floor area or fixed proportions is straightforward.

48   *Minja Properties Ltd v Cussins Property Group* [1998] 2 EGLR 52, HC per Harman J.
49   [1986] 1 EGLR 70.
50   [1998] 2 EGLR 52.

Rateable value

2.55   Where a lease provides for the tenant to pay a proportion of the costs with reference to the rateable value of the premises, this means the rateable value from time to time, so that the tenant's proportion will vary according to any fluctuations in the relevant rateable value.[51] The rateable value is that at the date when the expense is incurred or paid.[52]

Fair proportions

2.56   Where a lease obliges the tenant to pay a 'reasonable part' or a 'fair proportion' of the costs of works to a block of flats this can never be more than the amount actually spent on the tenant's property. For example, where a lease obliged a tenant to pay a reasonable part of the costs of works to a block of flats, and the landlord replaced all the windows, it was reasonable for the tenant to pay the whole cost of the landlord replacing the windows in the tenant's flat.[53]

2.57   The phrase 'due proportion' is usually taken to mean a reasonable or fair proportion of the relevant charges.[54]

2.58   It appears to be possible to argue that the method of apportioning service charges between tenants may make those charges unreasonable. For example where the charges were apportioned by surface area of each unit but the amount of work done on each unit varied widely; 'the inequity of the cost apportionment under the terms of the leases (was) an additional factor contributing to the unreasonableness of the (landlord's) course of action.'[55]

2.59   Where there has been an unexpected change in circumstances, the courts (and, one presumes, the LVT)[56] will make considerable efforts to ensure that a fair proportion is paid. For example, where a lease provided that the cost of heating was to be apportioned according to floor area, and the circumstances changed as a result of the installation of a new heating system which served a greater floor area,

---

51   *Moorcroft Estates v Doxford* (1979) 254 EG 871.

52   (1979) 254 EG 871.

53   *Sutton (Hastoe) Housing Association v Williams* [1988] 1 EGLR 56.

54   *Hackney LBC v Thompson* [2001] L&TR 7.

55   *Re 18,56 and 66 Fenlake Road and 25 and 64 Christie Road, Bedford Stapleton and others v Bedford Pilgrims Housing Association* CAM/96/UT/SC/011.

56   *Re Burlesden Court, East Cliff road, Dawlish, Devon EX7 0BP* LVT/HA/00/10 although see *Re 9 Grange Bunglows, London Road , South Mertsham, Surrey L82/99/SY* for a case where an LVT declined to take this approach.

the Court of Appeal decided that a 'fair and reasonable' proportion should be paid with reference to the tenants' use of the system and not according to floor area.[57]

Reserve or sinking funds

2.60   A reserve fund (or sinking fund) is a fund into which tenants pay a regular sum of money to be used by the landlord to cover the costs of unusual, unexpected or emergency works. The idea being to spread the cost of works evenly over time. Such funds are a good idea and any lease which does not have provision for such a fund may leave tenants and landlords in the difficult position of needing to find a large sum of money at short notice in order to carry out necessary work. Variation of a lease (see chapter 7) to include a reserve fund provision is the most straightforward remedy.

2.61   Payments into reserve funds are treated as service charges and are therefore held on trust[58] and disputes over their payment may be the subject of an application to an LVT. The LVT cannot order payments out of reserve funds in respect of certain items although a county court could make such an order.

2.62   LVTs frequently hear applications for the appointment of a manager where one of the key allegations is that the current manager is failing to collect or manage the reserve fund contributions. LVTs take a very dim view of such a failure of management, which is considered to be one of the most serious management failures.[59]

Set-off

2.63   Sometimes tenants wish to raise the fact that their landlord had breached a covenant under the lease, and, as a result of damages suffered by the tenants, their service charge liability ought to be reduced.

2.64   Where the breach of covenant by the landlord is a breach of covenant to repair which has lead to an increased service charge bill, the tenant may raise this without necessarily pleading a set-off (see para 2.37).

---

57   *Pole Properties v Feinberg* (1981) 43 P&CR 121.
58   LTA 1985 s18(3)(b) and see para 2.78 below.
59   See, by way of example, *Re flats 1–5 Leamington Road Villas* LVT/AOM/104/ 005/97, LVT/SCC/014/017/098.

2.65   Where the breach of covenant has caused other kinds of damage, the tenant would need to plead a set-off. A set-off[60] is a situation where A has a liability to B and B has a closely connected liability to A, such that B can reduce his liability to A by the amount that A owes to B. A set-off is pleaded as a part of a defence in a civil claim.

2.66   For example, if a section of fence blows down and the landlord does not repair it immediately, considerable damage might then be caused by vandals breaking in and causing damage. If the landlord were to sue the tenant in a county court for failure to pay service charges, the tenant could set-off the cost of the damage caused by the vandals against any service charges owed.

2.67   It is far from clear whether it is possible for a tenant to plead set-off in an application before an LVT. Set-off affects the amount owed by a tenant to a landlord and the LVT is concerned with questions of payability of a service charge. The notion of payability may be developed so that it encompasses the notion of set-off although to date there have been no decisions of an LVT or any court on this point.

2.68   The only indication of judicial thinking that might be relevant to this question is in the cases on the relationship between historic neglect and payability[61] see para 2.37 above.

2.69   Two separate principles are clear. There is no doubt that the relationship between a tenant's claim for damages for breach of covenant and a landlord's claim for service charges is such that the doctrine of equitable set-off may be applied.[62] A tenant may not set-off a claim against a claim for service charges brought by a manager appointed by the court or the LVT.[63]

Limitation

2.70   One of the most common questions asked by tenants seeking to apply to an LVT is 'how many years' worth of service charges can I challenge?' There is nothing in any statute or regulation which expressly governs LVTs. Nor is there any provision which expressly restricts the period into which an LVT can enquire when determining whether service charges are payable under LTA 1985 s27A.

---

60   Strictly speaking an *equitable set-off.*
61   *Loria v Hammer* [1989] 2 EGLR 249, *Wandsworth LBC v Griffin* [2000] 26 EG 147, *Blocks 94–110, 123–139 and 152–168 Clayponds Gardens, Ealing, London W5,* LVT/SC/032/029/02, LVT/SCC/032/021/02.
62   *Filross Securities Ltd v Midgeley* (1999) 31 HLR 465.
63   *Maunder-Taylor v Blaquiere* [2003] 1 WLR 379, CA.

2.71 It has been suggested that the Limitation Act 1980 may apply to restrict the compass of the LVT's enquiry. The Lands Tribunal has been found to be a court for the purposes of the Limitation Act 1980[64] and it seems likely that LVTs will also be similarly governed.

2.72 Even if the actions before an LVT are governed by the Limitation Act 1980, there are several possible time limits which might apply to a LTA 1985 s27A determination. This question has recently been discussed by an LVT,[65] where the following possibilities were suggested:

1) The application is an application for recovery of a sum payable under an enactment.[66] This was rejected because an LVT quantifies a sum due under a lease, rather than ordering that a sum be paid under a statute.

2) An action founded on a simple contract (that is not one made by a deed).[67] This might be applicable in respect of tenancies that were not made by deed – in practice tenancies shorter than seven years. The tribunal thought that this would not apply to applications brought by tenants (who are not seeking to recover under the lease) but only to actions for recovery of service charges by landlords.

3) An action on a specialty (that is, a deed).[68] The LVT thought that this would not apply to a tenant, who is not trying to enforce their own covenant to pay service charges under the lease. A tenant will be seeking a LTA 1985 s27A determination for some other purpose, for example, to trigger the appointment of a manager (see chapter 8).

Even if an action by a tenant were to be considered an action on a specialty, the tenant would be seeking to trigger a restitutionary remedy for money paid under a mistake. Time will only start running for such a purpose when the mistake was or could have been discovered with reasonable diligence.[69] Most likely this would be the date of the determination of the LVT.

By contrast an application by a landlord would be an action on a specialty, because it is the first step on the way to enforcing liabilities under the lease. Service charges which are reserved as rent may be different and are dealt with below.

---

64 *Hillingdon LBC v ARC Ltd* [1989] Ch 139, CA.
65 *Re 3, 12, 23, and 29 St Andrew's Square etc* LON/00AW/LSL/2003/0027.
66 Limitation Act (LA) 1980 s9.
67 LA 1980 s5.
68 LA 1980 s8.
69 LA 1980 s32(1). *Kleinwort Benson Ltd v Lincoln CC* [1999] 2 AC 349, HL.

4) An action for the recovery of arrears of rent.[70] Where the landlord has brought an application under a lease for the recovery of service charges which are 'reserved' as rent, the limitation period would be six years from the date when payment first became due. This would have no application to an action begun by a tenant.

5) An action by a beneficiary under a trust.[71] As explained below at para 2.78, service charges are normally held on trust[72] for the tenants. The LVT thought that LTA 1987 s42 would only apply where a landlord had misappropriated the service charge money for its own use. In such a case, no limitation period applies. This provision would not apply where the landlord had merely been unreasonable in their expenditure of the money, because it would be difficult to say that they had converted the service charge to their own use.

6) The LVT thought that if tenants were trying to start the restitutionary process, then it might be appropriate to consider the equitable defence of *laches*. This is a defence which applies to any claim to an equitable remedy, where the applicant has delayed so long it would be inequitable to grant the remedy. The LVT appears not to have appreciated that restitutionary remedies can be both equitable and common law and *laches* would not apply to a common law restitutionary claim.

2.73   After considering all these options the LVT held[73] that an application by a tenant under LTA 1985 s27A did not come under any provision of the Limitation Act 1980. The consequence of which is that there is no statutory time limit for bringing an action.

2.74   Regardless of any statutory limitation period, claims which cannot be supported by evidence are almost certain to fail. The further back in time that tenants seek to go, the harder it is likely to be to find sufficient evidence to support a challenge to service charges from those periods.

2.75   The LVT made it very clear in *St Andrew's Square*[74] that it would not hesitate to use its power[75] to strike out as frivolous or vexatious or otherwise an abuse of process claims it would regard as being stale.

---

70   LA 1980 s19.

71   LA 1980 s21(1).

72   LTA 1987 s42.

73   *Re 3, 12, 23 and 29 St Andrew's Square etc* LON/00AW/LSL/2003/0027.

74   Ibid.

75   Leasehold Valuation Tribunals (Procedure) (England) Regulations 2003 SI No 2099 reg 11.

Limits on demands

2.76   LTA 1985 s20B states that all service charges must be demanded within 18 months of the costs being incurred or the tenant is not liable to pay them.[76] This does not apply if within the period of 18 months beginning with the date when the relevant costs in question were incurred, the tenant was notified in writing that those costs had been incurred and that he would subsequently be required under the terms of his lease to contribute to them by the payment of a service charge.[77]

2.77   The purpose of section 20B is to avoid the tenant being faced with a bill for expenditure of which he had received insufficient warning; it was not intended to prevent the landlord from recovering expenditure of which there had been adequate prior notice. Accordingly the section has no application where:

a) payments on account are made to the lessor in respect of service charges,

b) the actual expenditure of the lessor does not exceed the payments on account, and

c) no request by the lessor for any further payment by the tenant needs to be made or is in fact made.[78]

d) service charges are claimed as mesne profits.[78a]

Service charge contributions are held on trust

2.78   Where there are tenants of two or more dwellings, all service charges monies actually held by the landlord or their agent will be held on a trust for the provision of services and for the tenant as beneficiary.[79] This does not apply to sums which are claimed by the landlord but not yet paid by the tenant.

2.79   There are two advantages to this:

a) the money is safe from creditors in the event that the landlord becomes bankrupt or otherwise insolvent;

b) the landlord and their agent are subject to the ordinary duties of trustees in relation to the monies held and they will be liable for

---

76   LTA 1985 s20B. See *Westminster CC v Hammond* December 1995 *Legal Action* 19.

77   LTA 1985 s20B(2).

78   *Gilje v Charlegrove Securities (No 2)* July 2003 *Legal Action* 27; [2003] 36 EG 110.

78a   *Mohammadi v Anston Investments Ltd* [2003] EWCA Civ 981, [2004] HLR 8.

79   LTA 1987 s42.

breach of trust if the money is misappropriated or not adequately safeguarded or invested.

2.80   The sums paid by way of service charges must be held either as a single fund or, if the landlord thinks appropriate, two or more funds.[80] A landlord is well advised to use not just a separate fund but a separate bank account.

2.81   A trust is created wherever tenants of two or more dwellings are required to contribute to the same costs. For example, consider two blocks of flats A and B, which share a communal garden. Tenants of each block are required to contribute (1) to the costs of repair and maintenance of their block ('block costs'); and (2) to the costs of maintaining the garden ('garden costs'). In this situation there are three trusts: two trusts of the block costs and one of the garden costs.

2.82   The trust fund and any interest collected on the money must be used to pay costs incurred in connection with the matters for which the service charges were payable.[81] The service charge monies are not to be seen as an additional source of profit, with the landlord pocketing any interest.

Investment of trust funds

2.83   If the landlord wishes to invest the service charge monies they may do so only:

a) with the Bank of England;
b) with a UK-based deposit-taking business in an account which will yield interest;
c) with a building society in an account which will yield interest; or
d) in building society shares.[82]

Termination of the lease

2.84   Subject to any express terms in the lease to the contrary, each tenant's share in the residue of the trust is proportional to their relative service charge liabilities.[83] Where:

i) a single tenant's lease comes to an end, their share in the residue of any service charge trust is absorbed into that trust;

80 LTA 1987 s42(2).
81 LTA 1987 s42(3).
82 Service Charges Contributions (Authorised Investments) Order 1988 SI No 1284.
83 LTA 1987 s42(4).

ii) after the termination of one of the leases, there are no remaining leases, the trust fund becomes the property of the landlord.[84]

2.85 The provisions outlined above are implied into every lease and a clause which purports to create any trust which is inconsistent with the terms of LTA 1987 s42 is inapplicable except for any express trust created before 1 April 1989.[85]

2.86 Disputes under LTA 1987 s42 are determined by the county court and not the LVT.[86] In consequence, it would seem that an LVT cannot make a determination that a landlord has failed to comply with any of the terms of section 42, including that service charge monies have not been kept in a proper account.

Commonhold and Leasehold Reform Act 2002 reforms

2.87 Commonhold and Leasehold Reform Act (CLRA) 2002 makes provision for some radical changes to this regime, although, as yet, none of these provisions are in force. LTA 1987 s42A demands that service charge payments be held on trust in an 'authorised account.' This will be an account held with a financial service provider (most likely to be a bank or building society). The landlord must have informed the financial service provider that the payments are to be held on trust for the purpose of paying service charge costs.

2.88 Tenants will have the right to withhold payments where they have reasonable grounds for believing that their landlord is not holding the monies in an authorised account.[87] Tenants will also have the power to inspect relevant documents that relate to the landlord's discharge of their duty.[88]

2.89 When LTA 1987 s42A comes into force, the Service Charges (Authorised Investments) Order 1998[89] will probably be repealed and replaced by new rules made under section 42A.

2.90 The provisions of section 42A will apply to a situation where only one tenant is liable in respect of any costs.[90]

---

84 LTA 1987 s42(6) and (7).
85 LTA 1987 s42(8) and (9).
86 LTA 1987 s52(2).
87 LTA 1987 s42A(9).
88 LTA 1987 s42A(3).
89 SI No 1284.
90 CLRA 2002 Sch 10 para 15.

Unfair terms in lease agreements

2.91   The Unfair Contract Terms Act 1977 does not apply to lease agreements.[91] However, it has recently been decided[92] that the Unfair
Terms in Consumer Contract Regulations 1999, which implemented
the EU Directive 93/113/EEC, do apply to contracts in respect of interests in land. A full discussion of the regulations is beyond the scope
of this work, however, it is now clear that all tenants, both of public
authorities and private landlords, are entitled to the protection provided by the regulations.

2.92   The most important consequence of the regulations for our purposes, is that any term of a contract which is unfair (within the meaning of the regulations) is not binding on the consumer, in this case
the tenant.[93] A tenant would therefore be able to argue that if a service
charge were imposed by an unfair term of the lease, that service
charge would not be payable.

2.93   The regulations also provide that where a term of a contract is
capable of more than one interpretation, the interpretation most
favourable to the consumer should be adopted.[94]

---

91 *Granby Village (Manchester) Management Co Ltd v Unchained Growth plc* August
1999 *Legal Action* 23.
92 *Newham v Zeb* [2004] EWCA Civ 55.
93 Unfair Terms in Consumer Contracts Regulations 1999 SI No 2083 reg 8(1).
94 Ibid, reg 7(2).

Tenants' rights to information

Key points

- Tenants have rights to information about their service charges.
- At the moment tenants can demand a summary of relevant costs from their landlord.
- A summary must be broken down into 12-month 'accounting periods.' It must contain information about the cost of works done or to be done, how this is to be paid for, and the balance of the tenants' service charge accounts. In some cases it must be certified by an accountant.
- When the new provisions of the Commonhold and Leasehold Reform Act (CLRA) 2002 come into force, the landlord will have to supply the accounting information without being asked. There will also be a right to withhold service charges where the landlord refuses to provide the tenants with the information.
- Tenants may already request a 'management audit' whereby an auditor is empowered to inspect the landlord's financial accounts relating to the property.
- Recognised tenants' associations have additional powers of consultation, especially in relation to managing agents and can appoint a surveyor whose powers are similar to those of an auditor under a management audit.
- The landlord must provide the following information when asked: the name and address of the landlord; if the landlord is a corporation, the names and addresses of the directors and company secretary.
- If the landlord changes, the new landlord must inform the tenants of this fact.

Introduction

3.1   The Landlord and Tenant Act (LTA) 1985 gives tenants certain rights to obtain information from and about their landlord. The most important of these empower tenants to obtain information about the basis of their service charge bills and to inspect documents on which those bills are based. A new set of provisions, named the 'accounting provisions', is set to replace these rights when the relevant parts of the Commonhold and Leasehold Reform Act (CLRA) 2002 come into force, which is hoped will be in the Spring of 2005.

3.2   The two significant differences between the new and old provisions is that a landlord will be required to provide some information without it being requested and that if a landlord fails to comply with some of the provisions a tenant can withhold their service charges until they do. The onus is then on the landlord to take action. This chapter will deal both with existing rights and the new accounting provisions, making clear which are and are not yet in force.

3.3   Except where otherwise noted, the rights described in this chapter may be exercised by any tenant who is required to pay service charges and would be able to challenge those service charges in an LVT. That is all tenants except:[1]

a) tenants of local authorities, new town corporations and National Park authorities, except those on long leases; and

b) statutory tenants who do not have a variable service charge in their registered rent.

Information to be given to a tenant

3.4   The LTA 1985 requires that a certain minimum amount of information be made available to all tenants, whether or not they are liable to pay service charges and whatever the form of their tenancy. Failure to comply with these provisions without a reasonable excuse is a summary offence punishable by a fine.[2]

Identity of the landlord

3.5   All tenants have right to know their landlord's identity. A tenant may make a written request asking for the landlord's name and address, which may be made to anyone who demands, or the last person who received, any rent payable, or to anyone acting as agent for the landlord.

3.6   That person must then supply a written statement of the landlord's name and address within 21 days from receipt of the request.[3]

3.7   If, after a successful request for the landlord's name and address, a tenant discovers that the landlord is a corporation, he or she may make a request in writing for the name and address of every director and the secretary of the corporation.[4] Such a request may be made to

---

1   LTA 1985 ss26(1) and 27.
2   LTA 1985 ss1(2), 2(4), 3(3) and 3A(3).
3   LTA 1985 s1.
4   LTA 1985 s2(1).

any person who demands rent (but not anyone who has merely received it) or is acting as agent of the landlord. Within 21 days of receiving the request that person must respond with the relevant names or addresses.

Change of landlord

3.8   If the landlord sells their interest in the property to a new landlord, the new landlord has a duty to give notice of this in writing to the tenant within two months or on the next day that rent is payable, whichever is the later.[5]

3.9   Such a notice should indicate the new landlord's name and address. A former landlord will still be liable under any covenants with the tenant until they have given the tenant notice in writing of the new landlord's name and last-known address; or the new landlord has informed the tenant of the name and current address.[6]

Summaries of cost

3.10   It is often difficult to know, when faced with a service charge bill, on what basis it has been calculated. In particular it is rarely clear what sums have been invoiced to the landlord and what sums have been paid out. Without this information a tenant is in a poor position to challenge the service charges before an LVT.

Accounting periods

3.11   A tenant may request in writing that their landlord supply them with a 'summary of relevant costs' for the previous 'accounting period'.[7] An accounting period is 12 months long. If the service charge accounts are made up in 12-month periods then the previous accounting period will be the one that last ended before the request was made.[8]

3.12   If the service charge accounts are made up in periods not of 12 months then the relevant accounts will be for the 12-month period

---

5   LTA 1985 s3(1).
6   LTA 1985 s3(3A).
7   LTA 1985 s21.
8   LTA 1985 s21(1)(a).

ending on the date of the request.[9] For example, if the landlord makes up service charge accounts in two 6-month periods being January to June and July to December and a tenant makes a request for a summary of costs on 20 September 2004 the accounting period for the purposes of the act will run from 21 September 2003 until 20 September 2004. The landlord would therefore have to adapt their own accounts to give a summary of this period.

3.13   The summary of costs will summarise the costs that were incurred in that period, rather than the amounts that were payable by, or demanded from the tenant. Any cost, part or all of which has been, or will be, passed on to the tenant as part of their service charge bill, must be included in the summary. The focus is on cost to the landlord rather than amount payable by the tenant.

What a summary must contain

3.14   The summary must include:[10]

a) statement of any works in respect of which various grants of public money have been or are to be paid;
b) how the costs have been or will be reflected in demands for service charges;
c) a summary of whether any demands for payment have been made in respect of any of the costs (for example, as invoices from contractors) and if so whether any money has been paid;[11]
d) the total amount of money received by the landlord up to the end of the accounting period in respect of 'relevant dwellings' that is still standing to the credit of those tenants. That is surplus money that has not yet been spent on relevant costs.

3.15   Item (d) is obscure. 'Relevant dwellings' are defined as the dwelling belonging to the person asking for the summary and the dwelling belonging to 'a person whose obligations under the terms of his or her lease as regards contributing to relevant costs relate to the same costs'.[12] Here it is unclear whether 'relate to the same costs', means identical costs, or that the tenants of the dwellings contribute to some of the same costs.

9 LTA 1985 s21(1)(b).
10 LTA 1985 s21(5).
11 LTA 1985 s21(5)(b) and (5)(c).
12 LTA 1985 s21(5A).

3.16   This ambiguity is illustrated by the following example. Consider a small development consisting of two blocks, A and B, each of two flats. The leases of the flats require that the tenants contribute to the costs of their block and to the costs of a shared garden. Block A is larger and has higher upkeep costs than block B. As was explained at para 2.81 above, the landlord will be required to keep three separate trust funds, one for block A, one for block B and one for the garden. If a tenant in block B asks for a summary of relevant costs, are all the flats 'relevant dwellings', or are only the flats in block B?

3.17   In the first interpretation the tenant would be supplied with a single figure showing the aggregate of all the money standing to the credit of tenants in both blocks. This could be quite misleading as the block A fund has nothing to do with their service charges.

3.18   The second interpretation is no more helpful because it omits any payments made by tenants of block A in respect of the garden.

3.19   Neither interpretation seems to be useful and both conflict with the manner in which service charges are held on trust. This is unfortunate as an obligation to state the amount standing to the credit of each trust fund would be much more useful.

Certification of the summary

3.20   If there are more than four relevant dwellings, in order for the summary to be valid a qualified accountant (see para 3.35) must have certified that the summary is a fair summary complying with the requirements set out above and being sufficiently supported by accounts, receipts and other documents produced to them.

Request for a summary of costs

3.21   A request for a summary of costs may be made by the secretary of a recognised tenants' association that represents the tenant (who must consent to a request being made on their behalf), the summary should then be supplied to the secretary of the tenant's association.[13] The request may also be served on an agent of the landlord or a person who receives rent on behalf of the landlord, who must then forward it as soon as possible to the landlord.[14]

---

13 LTA 1985 s21(2).
14 LTA 1985 s21(3).

3.22   The landlord must comply with the request within six months of the end of the relevant accounting period or within one month of the request whichever is the later.[15]

Statements of account (not yet in force)

The need for reform

3.23   The principle defects of the existing system of requesting summaries of costs are:

a) It requires the tenant to be aware of the right and to be proactive about seeking the information.

b) The landlord may delay giving the information for some time after the end of the relevant accounting period which means that a tenant may have already paid for a service charge before they have sufficient information to know whether it might be reasonable.

c) Enforcement requires a criminal prosecution, something that will be beyond the capacity of most tenants. Though a local authority can bring such a prosecution they have no duty to do so and are likely to be unwilling to spend time and money on a private dispute. If the landlord is a local authority, there is not even the sanction of a criminal prosecution to enforce compliance.

CLRA 2002 reforms

3.24   When the accounting provisions of the CLRA 2002 come into force LTA 1985 s21 will be replaced by a new section 21 which introduces the concept of a 'statement of account'.[16] It is hoped that the statement of account and the rules which govern it will go some way towards remedying the deficiencies of the system of summaries of costs in the following way:

a) The onus will be on the landlord to provide a statement of account, which will be in much the same form as the existing summary of information, whether or not it is requested by the tenant.

b) The statement of account will have to be provided within six months of the end of the accounting period to which it relates.[17]

---

15 LTA 1985 s21(4).
16 In this section references to LTA 1985 s21 will refer to the new section 21.
17 LTA 1985 s21(2).

    c) If a landlord fails to comply with their accounting obligations, a tenant will be able to withhold paying a relevant part of their service charges until the landlord does comply.

3.25 Regulations which set out the precise form and content of statements of account have not yet been published. The differences that are required by CLRA 2002 are:

    a) Statements of account must always be certified by a qualified accountant, regardless of how many dwellings there might be contributing to the costs;[18] the Secretary of State will have the power to make exceptions from this requirement by regulation,[19] at the date of writing no such regulations have been made.

    b) Accounting periods may be for any period, selected by the landlord, that is no longer than 12 months.[20] This will give better transparency to statements of account where the leases provide for service charges to be calculated on a quarterly or half-yearly basis. The first accounting period begins on the first date on or after the date when CLRA 2002 s152 comes into force when a demand for payment of service charges is made to any associated dwelling.[21]

    c) The statement of account will have to show the total sum standing to the credit of the tenant and all 'associated dwellings' at the beginning and end of the accounting period.[22]

    d) The statement of account must be accompanied by a summary of rights and obligations of tenants of dwelling houses in relation to service charges;[23] it is anticipated that the form of such statements will be governed by regulation.[24]

3.26 The definition of 'associated dwelling' suffers from the same criticism as applied to the term 'relevant dwelling' under the existing law, and this part of the new provisions would appear to suffer from the same shortcomings outlined in the example in para 3.15 above. It is hoped that when regulations are made as to the form of statements of account they will clarify the position.

---

18   LTA 1985 s21(3)(a).
19   LTA 1985 s21(5).
20   LTA 1985 s21(9).
21   LTA 1985 s21(10).
22   LTA 1985 s21(1)(c).
23   LTA 1985 s21(3)(b).
24   LTA 1985 s21(4).

Withholding (not yet in force)

3.27   Where a landlord has not supplied a statement of account with respect to an accounting period or has supplied a statement of account which does not exactly, or at least substantially, comply with the statutory requirements the tenant has the right to withhold payment of some of their service charges.[25]

3.28   The amount they may withhold is the total of the amount standing to their credit for the relevant accounting period and the amount paid in that accounting period.[26]

3.29   Any provision of the tenancy which provides for non-payment or late payment of service charges has no effect during the withholding period,[27] which means that the tenant is protected from administrative charges for late payment and presumably from forfeiture for breach of covenant to pay service charges.

3.30   Once the landlord has supplied the relevant statement of account, or replaced a defective statement with one that exactly or substantially complies with the statutory requirements, the tenant may no longer withhold payment.[28] There is no prescribed period of grace for the tenant after the statement has been supplied, it appears that payment must be made immediately.

3.31   The landlord has the right to apply to an LVT to determine that they have a reasonable excuse for not having supplied a statement of account at all or having supplied one that did not properly comply with the statutory requirements.[29] It is unclear what use landlords will have for such a power since as soon as they properly comply with the requirements, and serve a complying statement of account on the tenant, the tenant is no longer permitted to withhold their service charges. Such a course of action would seem much speedier than an application to an LVT.

3.32   It would only seem to be useful to a landlord to make a LTA 1985 s21B application where there was no possibility of complying with the requirements. This might occur where some *force majeure* destroyed the relevant documentation (receipts and accounts) which would prevent any accountant certifying the accounts. It is unlikely

25   LTA 1985 s21A(1).
26   LTA 1985 s21A(2).
27   LTA 1985 s21A(5).
28   LTA 1985 s21A(3).
29   LTA 1985 s21A(4).

to be reasonable not to comply simply because the landlord's sloppy administration has mislaid the relevant supporting documentation.

Summary of rights and obligations (not yet in force)

3.33   When the accounting provisions are brought into force a landlord will also be required to serve a summary of the rights and obligations of tenants of dwellings in relation to service charges with any demand for service charges.[30] The form and content of such a summary will be set out in regulations which have yet to be published[31] though they are likely to be similar in form to the summary of rights and obligations that must be served with statements of account.

3.34   A tenant who has not been served with such a summary may withhold payment.[32] Again any provisions of the lease relating to non-payment or late payment have no effect during the period that the tenant withholds service charges.[33] There is no provision for a landlord to ask an LVT to dispense with this requirement, if a tenant is validly withholding service charges the only recourse for the landlord is to serve another demand this time with an accompanying summary.

Qualified accountants

3.35   For the purposes of certifying summaries of cost a qualified accountant is someone who is eligible for appointment as a company auditor under the Companies Act 1989 s25.[34] They must *not* be:

a) an officer, employee or partner of the landlord or, where the landlord is a company, of an associated company;[35]

b) a partner or employee of any such officer or employee;[36]

c) a managing agent of the landlord for any premises to which any of the costs covered by the summary in question relate or the state-

---

30   LTA 1985 s21B(1).
31   LTA 1985 s21B(2).
32   LTA 1985 s21B(3).
33   LTA 1985 s21B(4).
34   LTA 1985 s28(2).
35   LTA 1985 s28(4)(b).
36   LTA 1985 s28(4)(c).

ment of account relates;[37] or an employee or partner of any such agent.[38]

3.36   Where the landlord is one of the following public authorities:

- a local authority;
- a New Town corporation;
- a National Park Authority; or
- an emanation of the Crown;

then the qualified accountant may be an officer or employee of the landlord and may be a member of the Chartered Institute of Public Finance and Accountancy.[39]

Supporting accounts

3.37   Once a summary of relevant costs has been received (even if it has not been demanded under LTA 1987 s21(1)) by a tenant or secretary of a recognised tenants' association, the recipient may, within six months of receiving the summary, make a request in writing to the landlord to afford them facilities to inspect the accounts, receipts and other supporting documents and to take copies or extracts from them.[40]

3.38   The facilities for inspection must be made available within one month of the request being made and must be made available for at least two months.[41] No charge may be made for the inspection of documents[42] though a reasonable charge may be made for the taking of copies or extracts.[43] There is nothing to stop the landlord recovering the cost of making documents available for inspection as part of the service charge bill provided that the lease would allow them to do so.[44]

Inspection of documents (not yet in force)

3.39   When the accounting provisions of CLRA 2002 come into force LTA 1985 s22 will be amended to strengthen the rights of tenants in

37   LTA 1985 s28(4)(d).
38   LTA 1985 s28(4)(e).
39   LTA 1985 s28(6).
40   LTA 1985 s22(2).
41   LTA 1985 s22(4).
42   LTA 1985 s22(5)(a).
43   LTA 1985 s22(5)(b).
44   LTA 1985 s22(6).

respect to documentation on which their service charges are based.[45] A tenant will not have to wait until he or she has received a statement of account; he or she may request the accounts, receipts and other supporting documents as soon as the statement of account should have been served.[46] Such a request must be made within six months of receipt of a statement of account that exactly or substantially conforms with the statutory requirements, so that if a landlord persistently fails to supply such a statement the time limit will be accordingly extended.[47]

3.40   The tenant may either require the landlord to supply reasonable facilities for inspecting the documents, including facilities to take copies of them;[48] or a tenant may require the landlord to make copies of extracts from documents and then either send them to the tenant or afford reasonable facilities for their collection.[49]

3.41   The landlord must comply with the requirement within 21 days of receipt of the notice from the tenant.[50] The landlord may make a reasonable charge for complying with these requirements[51] except that they may not make a charge for making documents available for inspection,[52] although they may still treat the cost of doing so as part of the costs of management and if permitted to do so add them to the service charge bill.[53]

3.42   The right to inspection of documents may be exercised by the secretary of a recognised tenants' association on behalf of any tenant who consents to him or her doing so.[54] The secretary would then serve notice on the landlord and be afforded the facilities for inspection and/or copying. Failure of a landlord to comply with the right to inspection of documents without a reasonable excuse is a summary offence, punishable with a fine at level 4 on the standard scale.[55]

45   In this section references to LTA 1985 s22 will be to the amended section.
46   LTA 1985 s22(1)(a).
47   LTA 1985 s22(4).
48   LTA 1985 s22(1)(a).
49   LTA 1985 s22(1)(b).
50   LTA 1985 s22(6).
51   LTA 1985 s22(8).
52   LTA 1985 s22(7)(a).
53   LTA 1985 s22(7)(b).
54   LTA 1985 s22(2).
55   LTA 1985 s25.

Right to a management audit

3.43   In certain circumstances, tenants may appoint an auditor to conduct what is called a 'management audit'. The auditor will then be empowered to require inspection of supporting accounts or (after the accounting provisions come into force) documentation, just as would a tenant.

3.44   The auditor may be able to inspect further documents and is also empowered to inspect the common parts of the premises. A management audit is useful because if a landlord fails properly to comply with the auditor's requests, the auditor may obtain a court order requiring them to comply.

3.45   A management audit must be requested by a minimum number of 'qualifying tenants' – the number depending on the number of dwellings in the 'qualifying premises'. Where there are only two dwellings either or both tenants may request a management audit.[56] If there are more than two dwellings at least two thirds of the tenants must make a request.[57]

3.46   A 'qualifying tenant' is a tenant of a dwelling under a long lease that is not a business lease.[58] Each dwelling may have at most one qualifying tenant.[59] If a dwelling is sub-let on a long lease the superior tenant is not a qualifying tenant.[60] If a dwelling is leased to more than one person jointly they are treated as being jointly the qualifying tenant.[61]

3.47   The auditor, who must not be a tenant, must either be a qualified accountant (see para 3.35 above) or a qualified surveyor.[62] A qualified surveyor is a fellow or professional associate of either the Royal Institution of Chartered Surveyors or the Incorporated Society of Valuers and Auctioneers.[63] An auditor may appoint any person to assist them with carrying out the audit.[64]

3.48   An auditor has the same power to require the same facilities for inspection or copying of documents as does a tenant under LTA 1985 s22 (see para 3.37 above). After the accounting provisions of the

56 Leasehold Reform, Housing and Urban Development Act (LRHUDA) 1993 s76(2)(a).
57 LRHUDA 1993 s76(2)(b).
58 LRHUDA 1993 s77(1).
59 LRHUDA 1993 s77(3).
60 LRHUDA 1993 s77(4)(a).
61 LRHUDA 1993 s77(4)(b).
62 LRHUDA 1993 s78(4).
63 LRHUDA 1993 s78(5).
64 LRHUDA 1993 s78(6).

CLRA 2002 come into force, the power will be extended to allow an auditor to require that copies of documents be made and either sent to him or her or reasonable facilities be made to allow them to be collected.

3.49   The auditor's power is wider than that of a tenant because he or she may also make a request in respect of 'any other documents sight of which is reasonably required by him or her for the purpose of carrying out the audit.'[65]

3.50   In order to exercise the right to have a management audit, the auditor must give a notice to the landlord, which must be signed by all those tenants who are requesting the audit.[66] The notice must:[67]

a) state the name and address of each tenant;
b) state the name and address of the auditor;
c) identify the documents which the auditor requires to inspect, or copies of which the auditor requires; and
d) if the auditor is proposing to carry out an inspection of the common parts; state a date, which must be between one and two months from the date of giving notice, on which the auditor will be making the inspection.

3.51   Such a notice is duly given to a landlord if it is given to a person who receives rent on behalf of the landlord. Such a person must forward the notice immediately to the landlord.[68]

3.52   A notice in the same form may be given to any 'relevant person' requiring them to copy or afford inspection of documents. A 'relevant person' is any person who discharges any of the management functions in the relevant premises, or who applies any of the service charges, or who has a right to enforce payment of service charges.[69]

3.53   In response to a notice the landlord may respond by sending copies of requested documents, or affording facilities for their inspection or copying (as the case may be) or the landlord may give a notice objecting to the supply of documents, giving reasons for the objection.[70] The landlord may also either approve the date for the proposed inspection by the auditor, or propose an alternative date, which must not be later than two months from the date of the notice.[71]

65 LRHUDA 1993 s79(2)(b), or (when it is brought into force) s79(2A)(a).
66 LRHUDA 1993 s80(2).
67 LRHUDA 1993 s80(3).
68 LRHUDA 1993 s80(5).
69 LRHUDA 1993 s79(7).
70 LRHUDA 1993 s81(1).
71 LRHUDA 1993 s81(1)(c).

3.54   Where within two months of a notice, the landlord or any other person has failed to comply with any of its requirements,[72] an application may be made to a court for an order requiring compliance. Such an application must be made within four months of the date of the notice.[73]

Recognised tenants' associations

3.55   A recognised tenants' association (RTA) may act on its own behalf in requesting information from a landlord and has (at present) a number of additional rights in respect of consultation.

3.56   A tenants' association may be recognised by a notice given in writing by the landlord to the secretary of the association or by a certificate of a member of the local Rent Assessment Committee panel. A landlord may rescind a notice of recognition giving a minimum of six months' notice.[74] Any member of the Rent Assessment Committee panel may cancel a certificate.

3.57   Though the Secretary of State has a power to regulate the granting of certificates recognising an RTA no such regulations have been made. In practice the panels seem to be willing to recognise any properly constituted association. Appendix E sets out the process for the creation of an RTA.

3.58   A number of cases have occurred where a second RTA has been recognised in a block of flats. These have arisen after a collective enfranchisement and then subsequent sale of a number of the leaseholds. The blocks then consist of a mixed population of freeholder tenants and tenants with no interest in the freehold. Understandably these two groups have conflicting interests and when they cannot be reconciled the non-freeholder tenants have applied for recognition of their own RTA because the landlord-recognised association does not in their view properly represent their interests.

Consultation on managing agents

3.59   An RTA has the power to require a landlord to consult with them concerning managing agents by serving a notice in writing.[75]

---

72   LRHUDA 1993 s81(6).
73   LRHUDA 1993 s81(7).
74   LTA 1985 s29(2).
75   LTA 1985 s30B.

3.60   If there is not already a managing agent employed by the landlord, before any such managing agent is employed the landlord must serve on the association a notice specifying the name of the proposed managing agent, the obligations of the landlord which the managing agent will be discharging and a period of at least one month in which the RTA may make observations on the proposal.[76]

3.61   Alternatively if a managing agent is already employed by the landlord, the landlord must serve a notice which specifies the obligations of the landlord which the managing agent will be discharging and a period of at least one month in which the RTA may make observations in this case on the way the managing agent has been discharging their obligations and the desirability of them continuing to do so.

3.62   If the landlord proposes to appoint a new managing agent then the landlord must again consult with the RTA. As long as a manager is employed the landlord must consult with the RTA every five years informing them of any change in the obligations that are discharged by the agent and asking for observations.

3.63   An RTA can notify a landlord that it no longer wishes to be consulted in which case the landlord's duty to consult ceases. Where the landlord's interest becomes vested in a new landlord the RTA's notice will cease to have effect so that they will have to serve a fresh notice.

Appointment of a surveyor

3.64   Housing Act 1996 s84 empowers a RTA to appoint a surveyor, who must be a qualified surveyor in the same sense as for a management audit (see para 3.47 above). The appointment of a surveyor is straightforward and may be done by giving the landlord notice in writing. The surveyor ceases to be appointed if either the RTA gives the landlord notice to that effect or the RTA ceases to exist (which presumably encompasses an RTA that ceases to be recognised even if the association continues). The rights and powers of a surveyor are similar to that of an auditor appointed under the right to a management audit and are set out in Housing Act 1996 Sch 4.

76 LTA 1985 s30B(3).

CHAPTER 4

Consultation on service charges

continued

Key points

- The Commonhold and Leasehold Reform Act (CLRA) 2002 reformed the nature of a landlord's duties to consult. The old rules are still relevant for any work carried out between 1 April 1986 and 30 October 2003.
- A landlord must consult where work is done which would require a tenant to contribute more than £250 in any 12-month 'accounting period.'
- A 'qualifying long-term agreement' (QLTA) is an agreement made on behalf of the landlord for a period of over 12 months.
- If a tenant would have to contribute more than £100 to the cost of a QLTA in any accounting period the landlord must also consult before entering into the QLTA.
- It is possible to ask an LVT to dispense with consultation requirements.
- For agreements that are not QLTAs, the landlord must supply detailed information relating to the proposed project, including its estimated cost.
- A landlord must obtain at least one estimate from a party wholly unconnected with them. Any connection to a party must be disclosed.
- Certain public works must comply with public tendering requirements.
- Before entering into a QLTA, a landlord must serve a notice of intention to enter the agreement; invite representations from the tenants; and have regard to these representations.
- The landlord must then put at least two proposals (essentially 'quotes') to the tenants. One such proposal must be from a person wholly unconnected with the landlord. Again, tenants may comment on the proposals.
- A failure by the landlord to comply with his duties to consult tenants will not necessarily prevent the landlord recovering the costs incurred as service charges. At best, it will allow the LVT to 'cap' the amount which can be recovered.

Introduction

4.1   A tenant is at a great disadvantage when challenging the reasonableness of a service charge. If the work has been done badly a decision by an LVT that no service charge is payable in respect of it may be of little comfort.

4.2   It will also be difficult to show that the cost incurred by the landlord was unreasonable because the tenant will rarely be in a position to obtain quotations from alternative contractors who are unlikely to go to the trouble of quoting for work that has already been done by someone else.

4.3   In order to put tenants on a more equal footing, landlords are required to go through a process of consultation with tenants concerning agreements they make for the maintenance of the premises in which the tenants live or for work to be done. This process will usually allow the tenants to suggest alternative contractors from whom the landlord will be required to obtain quotations.

4.4   Tenants' advisers should always check that a landlord has carried out the proper consultation process. It is important to understand that a failure to properly consult will not prevent any service charges being recovered: instead the tenants will be liable only for a capped sum. Under some circumstances (for example, where the work needed to be done urgently) the LVT may allow a landlord to recover service charges even where they have not properly consulted. A failure to consult is not decisive.

The law before CLRA 2002

4.5   Before the changes made by the Commonhold and Leasehold Reform Act (CLRA) 2002 came into force landlords were required to consult on any works that would exceed a cost threshold (see para 4.13). Failure to consult with tenants would mean that only that cost threshold could be recovered.

Changes made by CLRA 2002

4.6   The consultation process for works is now for the most part more onerous. In particular it will usually take longer and may require the landlord to obtain quotations from contractors nominated by tenants.

4.7   The second change applies to large public contracts, mostly undertaken by central or local government, where there is already a requirement to carry out a public tendering process. Less is required by way of consultation with tenants for such contracts on the assumption that the strict tendering rules will give them ample protection.

4.8   Third, most agreements for more than a year (called 'qualifying long-term agreements' (QLTAs)) entered into by a landlord for the management of the property will need to be consulted on with the tenants.

4.9   Work may be done under a QLTA using a much simpler consultation process again on the assumption that the agreement will already have been the subject of proper consultation.

4.10   Lastly the power to dispense with these requirements will now lie with an LVT rather than with the court. This is an exclusive jurisdiction. Landlords who wish to be relieved of their responsibility to consult will have to make an application to the LVT Service even if litigation concerning the relevant service charges is before a county court.

Old consultation requirements

Applicability

4.11   Before its amendment by CLRA 2002,[1] the Landlord and Tenant Act (LTA) 1985 s20 set out rules (the old consultation rules) for consultation by the landlord in respect of works to the building. The old consultation rules applied to any work done from 1 April 1986 to 30 October 2003 and to certain works done after that date (see para 4.76 below) whose cost exceeds a cost threshold.

4.12   The old consultation rules are still of importance because applications will continue to be made to LVTs in respect of work done before the new rules came into force.

4.13   The cost threshold under the old consultation rules for works done on or after 1 April 1986 but before 1 September 1988 is the greater of £500[2] or £25 multiplied by the number of dwellings let to the tenants concerned.[3] For work done on or after 1 September 1988 the cost threshold is the greater of £1,000[4] or £50 multiplied by the number of tenants liable to pay the relevant service charge.

---

1   CLRA 2002 s151.
2   LTA 1985 s20(3)(b) (unamended).
3   LTA 1985 s20(3)(a) (unamended).
4   LTA 1985 s20(3)(b), as amended by the Service Charge (Estimates and Consultation) Order (SCO) 1988 SI No 1285.

Consultation procedure under the old rules

4.14   If there is a recognised tenants' association (RTA) the landlord must send a notice to the secretary of the association together with a specification of the work to be done and give a reasonable time for the association to propose names from whom estimates should be obtained by the landlord.[5]

4.15   After allowing a reasonable time for proposals for estimates from a tenants' association the landlord must obtain two estimates for the work, at least one of which must be wholly unconnected with the landlord.[6] A copy of any estimates must be sent to the secretary of any tenants' association.[7]

4.16   A notice must then be sent to all tenants or displayed in a place where it is likely to come to the attention of all tenants, together with the estimates, inviting them to make observations by a specified date[8] which must be no earlier than one month from the date of the notice.[9]

4.17   Tenants who are represented by a RTA must also be told of their right to inspect a detailed description of the estimates and to take copies[10] though the landlord may have the right to recover any costs so incurred through the service charge.

4.18   The landlord is required to have regard to any observations made by the tenants.[11] It is unclear to what extent this imposes any real constraint on the landlord but it is likely to be interpreted as a very weak obligation. A landlord might fall foul of it if they were to act in a way that would prevent them having possible regard to observations made by the tenants, for example by making binding contracts for work with contractors before the receipt of an observation.

Urgent work exception

4.19   Where the work is urgent, the work be commenced before the expiry of the date given in the notice to tenants.[12] This means that a failure to wait one month for tenants to make observations will not necessarily breach the consultation requirements. Given that some concession is

---

5   LTA 1985 s20(5)(a).
6   LTA 1985 s20(4)(a) and (5)(b).
7   LTA 1985 s20(5)(c).
8   LTA 1985 s20(4)(b) and (c).
9   LTA 1985 s20(4)(d).
10   LTA 1985 s20(5)(d)(iii).
11   LTA 1985 s20(4)(e) and (5)(g).
12   LTA 1985 s20(4)(e).

made for urgent work in the consultation process, it would seem that a landlord should still serve the proper notice on the tenants even if there is no possibility of waiting a full month before starting work.

New consultation requirements

4.20 Under the new regime, there are potentially two stages at which a landlord may need to consult with tenants. In the first place, most agreements made by a landlord for more than a year will now be called Qualifying Long-Term Agreements (QLTAs). Before the landlord enters such an agreement, various consultation processes are prescribed. Should the landlord fail to consult, the amount of cost under the agreement that they can recover from a tenant will be capped. In addition, a landlord will still have to consult with tenants before undertaking any work on the building or premises, which is called 'qualifying work'. Failure to consult on qualifying work will result in the amount of the costs of work which can be recovered in a tenant's service charges being capped. This part of the chapter introduces a number of concepts common to all consultation requirements. It then defines QLTAs and outlines the consultation requirements appropriate to them and then deals with the consultation on qualifying works.

Cost thresholds

4.21 With respect to qualifying works, the Service Charges (Consultation Requirements) (England) Regulations (Consultation Regs) 2003[13] apply where the costs result in the relevant contribution of any tenant being more than £250.[14] If the consultation requirements are not complied with or a dispensation given by the LVT (see para 4.67) then the relevant contribution of every tenant will be capped at £250.

4.22 For QLTAs the cost threshold is based on the relevant contribution within an 'accounting period'. 'Accounting periods' are all 12 months long. If service charge accounts are made up to any other length, accounting periods run from 30 October to 29 October in the following year starting with 30 October 2003. If service charge accounts are made up for 12-month periods the first accounting period is the first one that starts on or after 30 October 2003.

13 SI No 1987.
14 Consultation Regs 2003 reg 6.

4.23   This means that there may be a period starting on 30 October 2003 and ending at some point before 30 October 2004 which is not part of any accounting period. This period of time would appear to be disregarded by the regulations so that regardless of what a tenant's contribution is within that period the consultation requirements will not be engaged.

4.24   The cost threshold for QLTAs is £100 in any accounting period.[15] Given that this is a relatively small amount and it may be difficult to predict in advance if any tenant's contribution will go above this level a landlord should make every effort to consult on a QLTA in advance.

Inspection of information

4.25   Many of the notices required as part of the consultation process require the landlord to supply detailed information, for example concerning estimates and details of work that needs to be done. The landlord has the option, rather than sending the information with the notice, to indicate a place where the information can be inspected and hours when inspection may take place.[16] Both the place and the hours for inspection must be reasonable.[17] No charge may be made for the inspection.[18] The landlord must enable copies to be taken or supply to the tenant on request, and for no charge, a copy.[19]

4.26   The regulations do not specify that the copying facilities need be free of charge, though it seems to be the intention of the regulations. There is nothing to prevent a landlord recovering the cost of providing such information as part of an administration charge (see chapter 6) which, of course, will have to be reasonable.

Connection to the landlord

4.27   Another feature common to the consultation procedures is the idea of a person connected to the landlord. In some cases a landlord will need to obtain at least one estimate from a person wholly unconnected with them and in other cases they will have to indicate if there is a connection (and what that connection is) between them and a party to an agreement.

---

15   Consultation Regs 2003 reg 4.
16   As provided for in Consultation Regs 2003 Schs 1–3 para 2(1) and Sch 4.
17   Consultation Regs 2003 Schs 1–3 para 2(1)(a).
18   Consultation Regs 2003 Schs 1–3 para 2(1)(b).
19   Consultation Regs 2003 Schs 1–3 para 2(2).

4.28   There is no exhaustive definition of what 'connection' means and a common-sense approach is likely to be taken by the LVT. The purpose of having such a concept is to increase the transparency of the consultation and tendering process.

4.29   Some relationships are deemed to be a connection and they are:[20]

a) A company is connected to its directors and managers and their close relatives.

b) A company is connected to any other company if any of its directors or managers is, or is to be a director or manager of the other company.

c) A company is connected to a partner in a partnership if any partner in the partnership is a director or manager of the company or is a close relative of such a director or manager.

This list is in no way exhaustive and there are certain to be many other situations where a connection will be found.

Close relative

4.30   For the purposes of the regulations a person's 'close relative' is a person's spouse, cohabitee, parent, parent-in-law, son, son-in-law, daughter, daughter-in-law, brother, brother-in-law, sister, sister-in-law, step-parent, step-son or step-daughter.

4.31   A person's cohabitee is either a person of the opposite sex who is living with that person as a husband or wife or a person of the same sex living with that person in a relationship which has the characteristics of the relationship between husband and wife.[21]

Public notice

4.32   Certain large public works or other agreements are required to be opened to a public tendering process.[22] For works or agreements that would fall under these regulations a landlord is not required to collect estimates from contractors nominated by tenants because the selection of the contractor is already governed by the regulations.

---

20 Consultation Regs 2003 Sch 1 para 5(6), Sch 2 para 4(3), Sch 4, Pt 1, para 4(3), Sch 4, Pt 2, para 4(7).

21 Consultation Regs 2003 reg 2(1).

22 Public Works Contracts Regulations 1991 SI No 2680, Public Services Contracts Regulations 1993 SI No 3228, Public Supply Contracts Regulations 1995 SI No 201.

4.33   The disadvantage to tenants of these provisions is that there is no duty owed to them under the regulations. If the tendering process is carried out in a defective fashion so that an unnecessarily expensive contractor is selected, tenants have no obvious form of redress.

Estimation of costs

4.34   In order for the consultation process to be realistic the landlord will have to give an estimate of the cost of the work. Where public notice is required, this may not be practical and the following approach is adopted.

4.35   Where it is practical for the landlord to estimate the relevant contribution of each tenant's unit of occupation then that estimate should be given.[23] Where it is not practical to do that but it is practical to estimate the total amount of expenditure on the building or other premises to which either the agreement relates, or on which the work is being done, then that estimate should be given.[24] Failing that, if it is practical to give the current unit cost or hourly or daily rate that would apply to any works to be done then that rate should be given.[25]

4.36   Where it is not practical for the landlord to give any of this information they must explain why they are unable to comply and give a date by when they expect to be able to supply the estimated amount, cost, or rate as the case may be.[26]

Right-to-buy tenancies

4.37   Certain statutes[27] allow a public sector tenant to purchase a lease of their dwelling from their public sector landlord. The resulting tenancy is called a right-to-buy tenancy.

4.38   For the first 30 days of a right-to-buy tenancy the consultation requirements do not apply.[28]

---

23 Consultation Regs 2003 Sch 1 para 5(7), Sch 2 para 4(4), Sch 4, Pt 1, para 4(4).
24 Consultation Regs 2003 Sch 1 para 5(8), Sch 2 para 4(5), Sch 4, Pt 1, para 4(5).
25 Consultation Regs 2003 Sch 1 para 5(9), Sch 2 para 4(6), Sch 4, Pt 1, para 4(6).
26 This saving provision is only available in Schedules 2 and 4, Pt 1. See Consultation Regs 2003 Sch 2 para 4(7), Sch 4, Pt 1, para 4(7).
27 Housing Act 1985 ss138 and 171A; Housing Act 1996 s16.
28 Consultation Regs 2003 regs 5(3) and 7(5).

Qualifying long-term agreements

Introduction

4.39   Commonhold and Leasehold Reform Act (CLRA) 2002 introduced the concept of a qualifying long-term agreement (QLTA). By entering into a QLTA a landlord can avoid detailed consultation over works done under the agreement. However, a landlord will be required to have consulted on the QLTA in the first place.

4.40   As will become apparent as a result of the transitional arrangements, certain other kinds of agreement (see para 4.76 below), which are not QLTAs, will also provide a landlord with the benefit of the abbreviated consultation requirements.

What is a QLTA?

4.41   A QLTA is any agreement made by or on behalf of a landlord or superior landlord for a period of more than 12 months[29] (so an agreement for one year is not a QLTA) subject to a number of exceptions. A very common example of a QLTA would be a contract to manage the property.

Agreements which are not QLTAs

4.42   Contracts of employment are excluded.[30] Management agreements made between a local housing authority and either a tenant management organisation or a body established under Local Government Act 2000 s2,[31] which provides for joint management by more than one local government body are not QLTAs.

4.43   Also not a QLTA is an agreement if the parties to the agreement are a holding company and one or more of its subsidiaries; or two or more subsidiaries of the same holding company.[32]

4.44   An agreement entered into when there are no tenants in the building or other premises to which the agreement relates is not a QLTA provided the agreement does not exceed a term of five years.[33]

---

29 CLRA 2002 s20ZA(2).
30 Consultation Regs 2003 reg 3(a).
31 Consultation Regs 2003 reg 3(b).
32 Consultation Regs 2003 reg 3(c).
33 Consultation Regs 2003 reg 3(d).

4.45   Two further exceptions are transitional in nature:

- an agreement made before 30 October 2003 for longer than 12 months; or
- an agreement under which works are to be done and public notice for those works was given before 30 October 2003 is not a QLTA.

As a result there is no penalty on a landlord for having failed to consult before entering into such an agreement.

Consultation requirements: QLTAs

Notice of intention to enter into an agreement

4.46   The landlord must give notice in writing of their intention to enter into the agreement[34] to each tenant[35] and to any recognised tenants' association.[36] The notice must:

a) Describe, in general terms, the 'relevant matters' (that is the subject matter of the agreement) or specify a place where a description of them can be inspected.[37]

b) State the landlord's reasons for considering it necessary to enter into the agreement.[38]

c) If the relevant matters include qualifying works, state the landlord's reasons for considering it necessary to carry out those works.[39]

d) Invite the making – in writing – of observations in relation to the proposed agreement[40] specifying the address to which observations may be sent, that they must be within the relevant period; and the date on which the relevant period ends.[41] This seemingly technical requirement is very important: without it a tenant might not realise the urgency of making a response. Tenant advisers should argue strongly against a landlord's request for a retrospective dispensation for failure to specify the time limit properly if a tenant has been prejudiced by it.

---

34   Consultation Regs 2003 Schs 1 and 2 (the QLTA Schedules) para 1(1).
35   QLTA Schedules para 1(1)(a).
36   QLTA Schedules para 1(1)(b).
37   QLTA Schedules para 1(2)(a).
38   QLTA Schedules para 1(2)(b).
39   QLTA Schedules para 1(2)(c).
40   Consultation Regs 2003 Sch 1 para 1(2)(d) and Sch 2 para 1(2)(e).
41   Consultation Regs 2003 Sch 1 para 1(2)(e), and Sch 2 para 1(2)(f).

e) If public notice is required for the agreement, state that the reason why the landlord is not inviting recipients to nominate persons from whom they should try to obtain an estimate is that public notice of the relevant matters is to be given.[42] Otherwise, if public notice is not required for the agreement, invite each tenant and any tenants' association to propose within the relevant period, the name of a person from whom the landlord should try to obtain an estimate in respect of the relevant matters.[43]

Observations

4.47 The landlord must 'have regard to' any observations made in the relevant period. Similar language was used in the old LTA 1985 s20 consultation requirement (see para 4.18). 'Have regard to' would seem not to impose any real duty on the landlord, though the landlord may be required to explain what their response is to any of the observations.

Estimates

4.48 For those agreements which do not require public notice, the notice will have invited tenants and tenants' associations to nominate a person from whom an estimate in respect of the relevant matters should be sought. The intention of the regulations seems to be that the landlord should be required to obtain quotations from at least one person nominated by a tenant and at least one nominated by a tenants' association. As will be explained, the regulations are unclear whether this effect has been achieved.

1) Where a single nomination is made by one tenant then the landlord should obtain an estimate from the person so nominated.[44]
2) Where several tenants each make a single nomination, a simple principle of majority selection is applied: the landlord must obtain a nomination from the person who received the most votes.[45]
3) Where more than one person receives the most votes (that is, there is a tie for first place) the landlord may choose to obtain an estimate from any one of the persons who came top.[46]

---

42 Consultation Regs 2003 Sch 2 para 1(2)(d).
43 Consultation Regs 2003 Sch 1 para 1(3).
44 Consultation Regs 2003 Sch 1 para 4(2).
45 Consultation Regs 2003 Sch 1 para 4(3)(a).
46 Consultation Regs 2003 Sch 1 para 4(3)(b) and (c).

4.49   Oddly this principle of 'majority' is abandoned if any tenant nominates more than one person. It would seem that the regulations intend the landlord to be able to select any person nominated by a tenant under these circumstances.

4.50   In fact this limb of the regulations only comes into play where a tenants' association has also made more than one nomination – the circumstance of one tenant making many nominations and a tenants' association making none is not envisaged.[47]

4.51   The regulations also make the implicit assumption that there is only one recognised tenants' association in any block. This need not be the case (see para 3.58 above).

4.52   Even if an LVT were to assume the regulations were intended to require that a landlord obtained an estimate from at least one person nominated by a recognised tenants' association, a landlord could subvert the process by recognising their own association (which they have the power to do) which might contain only one tenant. This association could then nominate any person of the landlord's choosing. There does not appear to be any way to prevent an unscrupulous landlord taking advantage of these loopholes.

Preparation of proposals

4.53   The next step is for the landlord to put together their proposals. In circumstances where public notice was not required there are further conditions:

a) There must be at least two proposals.[48]

b) One proposal must be that the goods or services are provided or the works carried out by a person wholly unconnected with the landlord.[49]

c) Where the landlord has obtained estimates from parties nominated earlier in the consultation process there must be a proposal based on that estimate (which might well also fulfil the condition of being wholly unconnected with the landlord).[50]

A proposal must also state:[51]

a) The name and address of all other parties to the proposed agree-

---

47 Consultation Regs 2003 Sch 1 para 4(4).
48 Consultation Regs Sch 1 para 5.
49 Consultation Regs Sch 1 para 5(2).
50 Consultation Regs Sch 1 para 5(3).
51 Consultation Regs Sch 1 para 5, Sch 2 para 4.

ment and of any connection (see para 4.27) between the party and the landlord.

b) An estimate of the relevant costs or rate must be given as explained at para 4.34 above.

c) If the landlord proposes to appoint an agent to undertake some of the landlord's duties then the proposal must state whether the proposed agent is or is not a member of a professional body or trade association and whether he or she subscribes to any code of practice or voluntary accreditation scheme relevant to his or her function.

d) It will be usual for any agreement made by a landlord to contain provisions for the variation of the amount to be paid or the manner in which it will be determined. For example this might allow for possible changes in circumstances of the property. Where public notice is not required (ie, under schedule 1) each proposal must contain a statement of any such provisions.[52]

e) The intended duration of the proposed agreement.

f) Where observations have been made before the relevant date (to which the landlord will have to have had regard) the landlord must summarise the observations and set out their response to them.

4.54   Having prepared the proposal the landlord must give notice in writing of the proposal to each tenant and to any recognised tenants' association. The proposal may either be sent with the notice or made available for inspection at a specified place within specified hours. The notice must invite the making of further observations by tenants on the proposals.[53]

4.55   Where public notice is not required (ie, under schedule 1), if the landlord enters into an agreement with someone who was neither nominated by a tenant or tenants' association nor submitted the lowest bid, they must, within 21 days of entering into the agreement:[54]

a) give their reasons for entering into the agreement

b) respond to any observations.

Where public notice is required (ie, under schedule 2), the landlord must, within 21 days of receiving an observation to which they must have regard, respond in writing to the person who made the observation.[55]

52 Consultation Regs Sch 1 para 5(11).
53 Consultation Regs Sch 1 para 6, Sch 2 para 5.
54 Consultation Regs 2003 Sch 1 para 8.
55 Consultation Regs 2003 Sch 2 para 7.

Consultation requirements: qualifying works

4.56   Consultation on qualifying works follows a very similar pattern to that for QLTAs but here there are three possible situations to consider:

a) Work done under a QLTA (or certain other agreements (see para 4.76)) is covered by Consultation Regs 2003 Sch 3 which provides for a very minimal consultation process.

b) Work that is not covered by an agreement is covered by Consultation Regs 2003 Sch 4.

c) Consultation Regs 2003 Sch 4 Part 1 applies to work for which public notice is required and Schedule 4 Part 2 for work which no public notice is required.

Notice of intention

4.57   The first step is for the landlord to give a notice of their intention to do the works. The notice is in the same form as that described at para 4.46 above for QLTAs except that for work covered by Consultation Regs 2003 Sch 3 and Sch 4 Part 1 the notice must also include the total estimated expenditure. For Sch 4 Part 2, no estimate of expenditure need be provided.

4.58   A 'qualifying date' must be given by when all observations and nominations of contractors (if invited) should be received. The landlord is required to 'have regard' to any observations received before the qualifying date.

4.59   All that needs to be done under Consultation Regs 2003 Sch 3 is to respond to any observations received within 21 days of their receipt. A response should be made in writing to the person who made the observation.[56] No further consultation with tenants is required.

4.60   Where the works are ones for which public notice is not required the landlord will have invited tenants to nominate persons from whom estimates should be collected. The rules for selecting persons from whom estimates should be obtained are worded slightly differently to those for QLTAs, although the differences are unlikely to have any material effect and do nothing to reduce the ambiguity already outlined.

4.61   The landlord must then produce a statement, called a 'paragraph 4 statement' when public notice is required and a 'paragraph (b) statement' otherwise.

56   Consultation Regs 2003 Sch 3 para 4.

4.62   Where public notice is required the landlord should already have chosen the party with whom they will be making the agreement and so the paragraph 4 statement need only set out who this party is. The statement must set out the name and address of the party and any connection (see para 4.27 above) that the landlord has with that party.

4.63   A paragraph 4 statement must also contain an estimate of the relevant cost (see para 4.34).

4.64   A paragraph (b) statement must contain the amount specified in a number of estimates. The estimates must satisfy the following conditions:

a) there must be at least two;
b) any estimate obtained from a nominated person must be included;
c) at least one of the estimates must be from a person wholly unconnected with the landlord. The landlord is under no duty to reveal any connection they have with any other parties from whom they have obtained estimates.

4.65   The paragraph (b) statement must also contain a summary of all the observations made in respect of the works and the landlord's response to them. All estimates must be made available for inspection.

4.66   The landlord must 'have regard to' any observations made within the relevant period after giving notice to the tenants and any tenants' association containing the paragraph 4 or paragraph (b) statement.

Dispensation

4.67   As explained above at para 4.21, where a landlord has not complied with the relevant consultation provisions, the amount they will be able to recover from a tenant will be capped at the relevant cost threshold. This can have harsh consequences in certain circumstances. The most obvious being:

• where there is a technical defect which does not prejudice tenants;
• where the work is of an urgent nature and there is simply not time to go through the consultation (recall that under the old rules, urgent work could be started during the consultation process, that is no longer true).

4.68   Under the old LTA 1987 s20 requirements the relevant dispensation provision is section 20(9), the new dispensation provisions are to be found in LTA 1987 s20ZA. There are two significant differences between the two provisions.

Jurisdiction over dispensation

4.69   In the first place LVTs have no jurisdiction to apply the old LTA 1987 s20(9) and so dispense with the consultation requirements under the old section 20 provisions. In the past LVTs had a very restricted jurisdiction over service charge disputes and could consider only their reasonableness (see para 2.9) in particular an LVT could not apply a cap under section 20. This meant there was no need for LVTs to be able to dispense with the consultation requirements.

4.70   Now that LTA 1987 s27A gives LVTs very general powers to decide the payability of a service charge they will be considering whether the former section 20 provisions have been complied with for some time to come.

4.71   A landlord may find themselves in the position of having a cap on the service charges applied by an LVT and having to apply to the county court under LTA 1987 s20(9).

4.72   Exactly the reverse situation applies to consultation under the new LTA 1987 s20 provisions. Here the court has no power to apply the dispensation under section 20ZA and so a landlord before the county court, where service charges are in issue in a case which would not be suitable before an LVT, the landlord will have to make a separate section 20ZA application to the LVT on this issue.

4.73   Tenant advisers should make this situation very clear to an LVT. The rules may be one-sided but they are advantageous to tenants.

Test for dispensation

4.74   The second distinction between the two dispensation requirements is that the old LTA 1987 s20(9) dispensation test was two-stage. First the court must satisfy itself that the landlord had acted reasonably and only then would it exercise its discretion to allow a dispensation.[57] The new test is that a tribunal may dispense if it is satisfied that it is reasonable to do so.[58]

4.75   As to the circumstances under which dispensation will be allowed: the reported cases on the old LTA 1987 s20(9) show a relatively restrictive approach and dispensation seems to have been confined to situations where urgent work was required.

57   *Seale v Maryland Estates Ltd* [1999] L & TR 541, CA (Robert Walker LJ and Blofeld J).
58   LTA 1987 s20ZA(1).

Transitional provisions

4.76 There are a number of transitional provisions that affect whether work is governed by the old or new regulations, and, if so, which Schedule of the Consultation Regs 2003 governs the work. The following table should provide a useful summary. In order to determine which consultation provisions apply start at the top of the table and work down.

Work done before 31 October 2003[59]	Old
A section 20 notice has been issued before 31 October 2003[60]	Old
A public notice was issued before 31 October 2003; the agreement under which the work is done was made on or after that date; and was for 12 months or less[61]	Old
Work carried out at any time between 31 October 2003 and 31 December 2003[62]	Old
Work done on or after 31 December 2003, pursuant to an agreement made before 31 October 2003[63]	Schedule 3
Public notice was issued before 31 October 2003 and the work was done on or after 31 October 2003 under an agreement for more than 12 months[64]	Schedule 3
Work done under an agreement for 12 months or less[65]	Schedule 4
Work done under an agreement made before 31 October 2003 and for more than 12 months[66]	Schedule 4
Work done under an agreement of more than 12 months duration, where public notice was given before 31 October 2003[67]	Schedule 4
Work done under any other agreement that is a QLTA[68]	Schedule 3
Work done in any situation not covered above[69]	Schedule 4

Key
Old   Covered by the former LTA 1985 s20
Schedules 3 & 4 Consultation Regs

59 Commonhold and Leasehold Reform Act 2002 (Commencement No 2 and Savings) (England) Order (CO2) 2003 SI No 1986 r3(3).
60 CO2 r3(4).
61 CO2 rr3(5), 3(6).
62 CO2 r3(7).
63 Consultation Regs r7(3)(a).
64 Consultation Regs r7(3)(b).
65 LTA 1985 s20ZA(2), Consultation Regs r7(4).
66 Consultation Regs r3(2).
67 Consultation Regs r3(3).
68 Consultation Regs r7(1).
69 Consultation Regs r7(4).

Insurance

Key points

- Disputes arise on one of three grounds:
  - If the lease contains no, or inadequate provision for insuring the property, consider varying the lease (see chapter 7).
  - If the landlord organises the insurance themselves and re-covers the cost of premiums from the tenant, the tenant will be paying for the insurance through his or her service charges (see chapter 2 for information on challenging service charges).
  - If the tenant organises the insurance but must use an insurer nominated or otherwise selected by their landlord, the tenant may challenge that choice of insurer; such a challenge is the subject of this chapter.
- Tenants may argue that the insurance cover is unsatisfactory in any respect or the premiums are excessive.
- 'Unsatisfactory' insurance includes situations where the level of cover is inadequate or excessive; there is a material misdescription which might lead the insurers to declining liability; or the cover is not provided by a reputable company.
- The phrase 'excessive premium' is not defined.
- Landlords often receive commissions from insurers. These are hard to challenge in themselves but can be used as evidence that the landlord is not negotiating at arms length in an open market.

Tips for advisers

- The tenants should prepare a list of possible insurance companies that they would be prepared to accept.
- Quotes must be 'like-for-like' if they are to be accepted as evidence of the landlord having overcharged.
- Depending on the insurance policy, a tenant may have the right to inform the insurer of any damage which could be the subject of a claim.

Introduction

5.1   A common area of dispute between tenants and landlords is the provision of insurance cover. This may flow from entirely legitimate differences of view, often from the fact that tenants, having time-limited interests in the property, take a different view of some risks when compared with freeholders. This chapter discusses the kinds of problems that might arise and how they might best be dealt with.

Common areas of difficulty

5.2 There are three ways in which a dispute about insurance can arise, all of which have different remedies.

No or inadequate insurance provision

5.3 Some leases make no provision for insurance or do not properly specify who is to insure particular parts of the building. In these circumstances tenants run the risk of having to pay for serious damage without any insurance protection.

5.4 Tenants are free to negotiate their own cover but there is a more satisfactory solution: that of applying for a variation of the lease, which is discussed in chapter 7.

Insurance premiums as service charges

5.5 A common situation is for a lease to put the duty to insure on the landlord, who is then permitted to recover the cost of the insurance premiums from the tenants. In such a situation the costs recovered from the tenants are service charges.[1]

5.6 Such payments are subject to the same kinds of challenge as other service charges, a full discussion of which may be found in chapter 2 at para 2.41.

5.7 A problem that arises in the particular instance of service charges for insurance is that landlords are often paid large commissions for selecting particular insurers. The insurance company then recovers the cost of the commission via higher premium payments which will ultimately be born by the tenants. The landlord will, by an indirect route, be profiting from the tenants, something they are not entitled to do. A full discussion of this particular problem is also found in chapter 2 at para 2.44.

---

1 Landlord and Tenant Act (LTA) 1985 s18.

Tenant required to insure

5.8   A further possibility is that the tenant is responsible for the insurance. This is particularly common for owners of leasehold houses. In such situations the lease almost always requires the tenant to use a particular insurer or one nominated by the landlord.

5.9   The landlord may collect the insurance premiums on behalf of the insurer. This may make it unclear to a tenant whether they are paying insurance service charges, or whether they are themselves responsible for the insurance and the landlord is merely an agent. There is a significant practical difference because the remedies available to the tenant are quite different in each case.

5.10   If the insurance payment is in fact a service charge, the remedies available are those discussed in chapter 2. If in the alternative the landlord is an agent, and it is the tenant who is contracting with the insurer, paragraph 8 of LTA 1985 Sch 1 gives either the landlord or the tenant the right to challenge the insurance cover as being unsatisfactory or the premium payments as being excessive.

5.11   The lease is determinative of whether a payment for insurance is properly a service charge or not. The main focus of this chapter is on applications under paragraph 8.

Challenging insurance cover

5.12   Where the lease requires the tenant to insure the property with an insurer nominated or approved[2] by the landlord then the tenant or the landlord may apply to an LVT for a determination of:

- whether the insurance which is provided is unsatisfactory in any respect; or
- whether the premium payments are excessive.[3]

5.13   There is nothing to prevent an applicant asking the LVT to rule on both questions in a single application.

5.14   Similarly, although this chapter describes this route as a remedy for an aggrieved tenant, there is no reason why a landlord could not bring an application and ask for a determination that the insurance is

---

2   'Approved' added by Commonhold and Leasehold Reform Act (CLRA) 2002 s165.

3   LTA 1985 Sch 1 para 8(2).

satisfactory and/or not excessively expensive. This may forestall any future disagreements between landlord and tenant.

Unsatisfactory in any respect

5.15 'Unsatisfactory in any respect' is not defined in the legislation, but is clearly a widely drafted provision. The following are examples of the most usual complaints.

Level of cover is inadequate or excessive

5.16 This would include situations where the policy fails to deal with a likely risk, or is simply far too cautious. A failure to insure against flood damage if the property were near a river prone to flooding would clearly be an example of inadequate cover. Similarly, while terrorism insurance might be appropriate for properties in larger cities, it may well be seen as excessive in respect of a cottage in an isolated, rural area.

5.17 Tenants should also ensure that the insurance policy provides for the property to be insured up to its re-build value. Though such a failure has never been raised before an LVT, it would seem to fall within 'unsatisfactory in any respect'. Were an LVT not to so accept, an application to vary the lease to this effect should be considered.

The cover is defective in some other respect

5.18 Examples include a material misdescription of the property in the insurance policy or other error which might lead to the insurers declining liability.[4]

The cover is not provided by a reputable company

5.19 There is a long line of case law to the effect that when a landlord has a covenant to insure the property, they must do so with an insurer of repute and good standing.[5] In practice, it should be considered adequate to insure with a firm of national repute.

---

4   *Re Blocks C, E and G, Cherry Blossom Close, Chequers Way, London N13* LVT/INS/027/003/00.
5   *Bandar Properties v JS Darwen* [1968] 2 All ER 305; *Havenridge Ltd v Boston Dyers Ltd* [1994] 2 EGLR 73; *Tredegar v Harwood* [1929] AC 72.

Excessive premium payments

A common confusion

5.20   As has already been made clear there is considerable confusion in the case law and literature between challenging a landlord-nominated insurer on the grounds of excessive premium payments and challenging the reasonableness of premium payments recovered as service charges. The two situations are quite distinct and will depend on a construction of the lease as to whether insurance is effected by the landlord or the tenant.

5.21   In particular, there has been a tendency to assume that case law that concerns the recovery of service charges applies equally to a challenge made to a landlord-nominated insurer.

Excessive from the tenant's point of view

5.22   Landlord and Tenant Act (LTA) 1985 s19, which governs the reasonableness of service charges, has been interpreted in a manner which focuses on the reasonableness of the landlord (see para 2.36). By contrast challenges to the landlord's nominated insurer on the grounds that a premium payment is excessive, focuses on the payment from the point of view of the tenant.[6]

5.23   It is common for landlords to cite the case of *Berrycroft Management*[7] as authority that if they have negotiated the insurance at arms length[8] in an open market, any premium payment will not be excessive.

5.24   *Berrycroft* is a service charge case and has no direct application to the challenge to a landlord-nominated insurer. To treat arms length negotiation as determinative of the question of whether premium payments are excessive, would be 'to emasculate the protection afforded to leaseholders by . . . paragraph 8 [of LTA 1985 Sch 1]'.[9] At best, arms length negotiations for an insurer is evidence which an LVT might take into account in deciding whether premium payments are excessive.

---

6   *Harker v Forcelux Ltd* M/INS/3, LVT.
7   *Berrycroft Management v Sinclair Gardens Investments* (1997) 29 HLR 444; [1997] 1 EGLR 47.
8   See glossary for explanation of the term 'at arm's length'.
9   *Re Blocks C, E and G, Cherry Blossom Close, Chequers Way, London N13* LVT/INS/027/003/00.

How much is excessive?

5.25   Premium payments are not excessive simply because they are not the cheapest. There is clearly a range of reasonable premiums available to any landlord and they cannot be faulted because they have not selected the cheapest available.[10]

5.26   As a rule of thumb, LVTs do not seem impressed by evidence from tenants that they could obtain a number of quotations at 20–30 per cent less than the premium imposed by the landlord's insurer. Conversely where the landlord's insurer is charging premiums over twice the size of quotations obtained by tenants, the LVT has almost always found those to be excessive.

5.27   When seeking to challenge the premiums, LVTs are entitled to use their local knowledge of the insurance market, but there is no common practice to this effect. Much more important is for tenants to obtain evidence of alternative like-for-like quotes.

Remedies

5.28   If an LVT finds the insurance arrangements to be unsatisfactory, it may make an order requiring the landlord to nominate an insurer specified in the order or requiring the landlord to nominate another insurer who will be capable of meeting the requirements listed in the order. Tenants are advised to bring evidence of the insurers they wish to see nominated and their reasons for so wishing.

5.29   Any agreement by the tenant (other than an arbitration agreement) which purports to provide for an alternative method of resolution or determination of insurance issues is void in so far as it would trespass on the rights of either party to make an application under paragraph 8.[11]

Other possible insurance problems

5.30   There have been reports of situations where a landlord refuses to apply money obtained as a result of a claim under an insurance policy. Such situations are comparatively rare, since a lease with an insurance provision should also contain a covenant to apply the sums received by way of insurance to the rebuilding or repairing of the

10 *23–45 The Woodfines, Hornchurch, Essex RM11 3HR* LVT/INS/030/003/99.
11 LTA 1985 Sch 1 para 8(6).

property. Insurance legislation often exists to overcome this problem, for example, Fire Prevention (Metropolis) Act 1774 s83 provides that a tenant may claim on their landlord's policy in respect of a fire.

5.31   If a lease does not contain a covenant in the terms suggested above then it should be varied. This should be done by agreement with the landlord but failing that an application to the LVT to vary the lease may be necessary (see chapter 7).

5.32   If the policy of insurance is taken out in the names of both the tenant and landlord they will be entitled to share any insurance payments in the same proportion as their respective interests in the premises. This may provide an alternative means to ensuring tenants are able to put insurance money back into the property.[12]

5.33   A third possible remedy in this situation is to sue the landlord for breach of covenant. Where a tenant pays a proportion of the premium of an insurance policy in favour of the landlord, the latter is obliged to exercise the rights conferred by the policy to protect the tenant's interest.[13]

Arranging your own insurance (not yet in force)

5.34   The following provisions are not expected to come into force until the Spring of 2005. Advisers should check carefully before seeking to rely on the following provisions.

5.35   Where a tenant has a long lease[14] of a house[15] and is required by the lease to insure the house with an insurer nominated or approved by the landlord, CLRA 2002[16] now provides that the tenant is not required to effect the insurance with the landlord's insurer if the tenant instead ensures that the house is insured under a policy of insurance with an authorised insurer.[17]

5.36   If a tenant chooses to take such a step, there are a number of guarantees which must be contained in the policy of insurance:

- the policy must protect both the interests of the landlord and the tenant;[18]

---

12   *Beacon Carpets v Kirby* [1984] 3 WLR 489; [1984] 2 All ER 726.
13   *Vural v Securities* (1990) 60 P&CR 258.
14   CLRA 2002 ss76 and 77.
15   As defined by Part 1 LRA 1967.
16   CLRA 2002 s164.
17   CLRA 2002 s164(2)(a), see also Financial Services and Markets Act 2000 s19.
18   CLRA 2002 s164(2)(b).

- the policy must cover all the risks which the lease requires to be covered;[19]
- the amount of cover must not be less than that which the lease requires to be provided by insurance.[20]

In addition, there is a strict procedure to be followed by any tenant thinking of taking this route.

5.37   The tenant must give the landlord a notice of cover. This must include the name of the insurer; the risks covered by the policy; the amount and period of the cover.[21] Also, the notice of cover must be served on the landlord within 14 days of the date on which it took effect or was renewed. In the case of a new landlord, the tenant may be requested to provide a copy of the notice of cover within one month and 14 days of the new landlord acquiring the interest of the previous landlord.[22]

5.38   If the notice of cover is to be posted to the landlord, it must be sent to the address specified by the landlord, either as the address for service of notices[23] or, if that is unknown, the address used for demands for rent.[24] Alternatively, the landlord may nominate an entirely different address in England or Wales.[25] It is strongly recommended that any such notice of cover be sent by recorded delivery.

Rights to information in relation to insurance

5.39   If a tenant or recognised tenants' association is faced with a service charge demand in respect of insurance, the tenant possesses certain additional rights to information.

5.40   The tenant should serve a letter requesting such information on either the landlord or his named agent or any person who receives rent on behalf of the landlord. Any person who receives such a request must pass it on to any superior landlord.[26]

---

19   CLRA 2002 s164(2)(c).

20   CLRA 2002 s164(2)(d).

21   CLRA 2002 s164(5) and (6) envisage both further information being required and a prescribed form being set out. As yet, there does not appear to be any such prescribed form, nor has any Statutory Instrument been enacted requiring additional information.

22   CLRA 2002 s164(4).

23   Landlord and Tenant Act (LTA) 1987 s48.

24   LTA 1987 s47.

25   CLRA 2002 s164(8).

26   LTA 1985 Sch 1 para 4.

5.41   The landlord can be required to provide a written summary of the insurance in respect of the property, setting out:[27]

- the amount insured under any relevant policy;
- the name of the insurer;
- the risks insured against.

5.42   Within six months of receiving such information, the tenant may require the landlord to allow him access to the original policy itself and any related accounts.[28] Copies of such documents may be taken.

5.43   Failure on the part of the landlord to comply with these duties is a criminal offence punishable by a fine.[29]

Right to notify insurer of a claim

5.44   Any tenant who pays a service charge in respect of insurance provision is also entitled to report any damage which may be subject of a claim under the insurance policy to the insurers.[30] However, this right is only exercisable if the insurance policy requires a person insured to give notice of any claim within a specified period. If this is the case, the tenant has the right, within that period, to contact the insurer in writing and specify the nature of the damage.

---

27 LTA 1985 Sch 1 para 2.
28 LTA 1985 Sch 1 para 3.
29 LTA 1985 Sch 1 para 6.
30 LTA 1985 Sch 1 para 7.

Administration charges

Key points

- Prior to the Commonhold and Leasehold Reform Act (CLRA) 2002, leases could provide for payments which were neither rent nor service charges. Some of these are now classified as 'administration charges'.
- An administration charge is one charged by a landlord in association with the cost of:
  - granting approvals
  - considering applications
  - providing information
  - failures by tenants to make a payment
  - breaches of covenant.
- Administration charges are either 'fixed' or 'variable.' If a sum is a set amount or calculated by reference to a formula, it is 'fixed', otherwise it is 'variable'.
- Leasehold Valuation Tribunals have the power to vary leases where 'fixed' charges are unreasonable. The variation is binding on all parties, including any successors to the lease. This remedy cannot be used to challenge sums which have already become payable.
- A tenant may apply to an LVT for a determination of the payability of an adminstration charge that was payable on or after 30 September 2003.
- 'Variable' administration charges are payable only to the extent that they are reasonable. This has the same meaning as 'reasonable' in the context of service charges.

Tips for advisers

- A tenant has the right to withhold any administration charges until the landlord provides a summary of the rights and obligations of the tenant in relation to those charges.

Introduction

6.1   Many leases provide for the recovery by the landlord from the tenant of various sums other than rent, for example a charge for late payment of rent. These were held not to be service charges and were therefore not within the jurisdiction of the LVT.[1]

---

1   *Forcelux Ltd v Sweetman* [2001] 2 EGLR 173.

6.2   Tenants found it more difficult to challenge such charges as they were unable to make use of an LVT. There was anecdotal evidence of abuse by unscrupulous landlords. Shedule 11 of Commonhold and Leasehold Reform Act (CLRA) 2002 has created a new legal category – the administration charge – which covers some of the most common of these additional charges.

6.3   An administration charge is one of:[2]

a) costs associated with the granting of approvals under the lease, or considering applications for such approvals, such as consent to alterations;

b) the costs of providing information or documents to the tenant or any other third party, such as would arise in connection with the sale of the leasehold;

c) charges arising out of a failure by the tenant to make a payment due under the lease;

d) charges arising from a breach or alleged breach of covenant.

6.4   Administration charges are divided into two classes:

a) Those which are fixed under the lease (for example, a fee of £50 for each late payment of a service charge) or calculated according to a formula specified in the lease (for example, by reference to the retail price index). These are often called 'fixed' administration charges though this is a slightly misleading name since they might well vary from year to year if they are calculated according to a formula.

b) Any other administration charge, which is known as a 'variable administration charge'.

Challenging fixed administration charges

6.5   The only remedy in respect of 'fixed' administration charge is to vary the lease. There is a special procedure for varying the terms of the lease that determine the amount of a 'fixed' administration charge. The procedure is quite distinct from that discussed in chapter 7 which allows a far more general variation of leases.

6.6   A party to the lease may apply to the LVT for an order varying the lease on the following grounds:[3]

• the administration charge specified in the lease is unreasonable, or

2   CLRA 2002 Sch 11 para 1(3).
3   CLRA 2002 Sch 11 para 3(1).

- any formula specified in the lease is unreasonable.

6.7   A 'right to manage' company[4] is treated as being a party to the lease for these purposes.[5]

6.8   There does not seem to be any reason why a landlord should not apply for the increase of a fixed administration charge provision in the lease that was unreasonably small. A court appointed manager would not be able to make an application of this kind because he or she would not be a party to the lease. He or she might be able to apply to an LVT to vary the terms of his or her appointment so that he or she is allowed to charge a suitable fee.[6]

6.9   As yet there is no guidance on how 'unreasonable' will be construed. It seems likely that the LVT will take a similar approach to that employed when dealing with service charges, and, as such, the test will be whether or not the charge is unreasonable from the landlord's perspective.[7]

6.10   The tribunal may, if it finds fault with a provision of the lease that provides for an administration charge, vary it as they see fit. This may take the form of endorsing the variation proposed in the application, but the LVT does expressly have a power to make any other variation as it thinks fit.[8] Alternatively, the LVT may direct that the parties to the lease make arrangements to have it varied in a manner as directed.

6.11   Any variation will be binding for the duration of the lease on the parties to the lease and any successors in title. Interestingly, predecessors in title are also bound by the variations.[9] The change only affects the payability of administration charges after the lease is varied.

6.12   If a fixed administration charge becomes payable, there is no remedy from an LVT for a tenant who wishes to dispute it, even if it is clearly unreasonable. He or she may have grounds for varying the lease but this will only affect future payments.

Payability of variable administration charges

6.13   The provisions that control variable administration charges mirror those already discussed for service charges (see chapter 2 above). In

4   See chapter 9.
5   CLRA 2002 Sch 7 para 16.
6   See para 8.27 below.
7   See para 2.36 above.
8   CLRA 2002 Sch 11 para 3(3).
9   CLRA 2002 Sch 11 para 3(6).

particular a variable administration charge is only payable to the extent that it is reasonable.[10]

6.14   As with service charges, an application may be made to an LVT to determine:

a) the person by whom the charge is payable;
b) the person to whom it is payable;
c) the amount which is payable;
d) the date at which it is payable;
e) the manner in which it is payable.

6.15   The procedure for any such application will closely follow that set out in relation to service charges. It is also likely that the discussions on 'reasonableness' in the service charge context will provide useful guidance for applications in relation to administration charges. See chapter 2.

6.16   As with service charges, the application may be made whether or not payment has been made, but not if the matter has been agreed or admitted by the tenant, has been referred to an arbitration process, or has been determined by a court or arbitration process.[11]

6.17   Any agreement by the tenant (other than an arbitration agreement) which purports to provide for an alternative method of resolution or determination of administration charges is void in so far as it would trespass on the rights of either party to make an application under Schedule 11.[12]

6.18   The right to challenge administration charges only applies to administration charges which became payable on or after 30 September 2003.[13]

Demands for administration charges

6.19   A demand for the payment of an administration charge must be accompanied by a summary of the rights and obligations of the tenants in relation to the administration charges.[14] No prescribed form of the summary notice has yet been drawn up by the Secretary

10 CLRA 2002 Sch 11 para 2.
11 CLRA 2002 Sch 11 para 5(4).
12 CLRA 2002 Sch 11 para 5(6).
13 Commonhold and Leasehold Reform Act 2002 (Commencement No 2 and Savings) (England) Order 2002 SI No 1986 art 2.
14 CLRA 2002 Sch 11 para 4(1).

of State. As long as the information is clear and understandable, in the absence of any prescribed form, the summary is likely to be acceptable.

6.20   A tenant has the right to withhold payment of administration charges until the summary of rights and obligations is provided to him or her.[15]

Estate management schemes

6.21   Where a group of tenants have bought the freehold, some land may remain in their former landlord's hands (for example, communal gardens or roads). It may be that this land needs money to be spent on it and the landlord will wish to recover the cost of maintaining the 'estate' from the former tenants. Such a system of freehold management is called an 'estate management scheme' (EMS) and the charges under the system being known as 'estate charges'.[16]

6.22   Unlike the situation with service and administration charges, where only charges for certain specified classes of cost are service or administration charges, any cost that an occupier or someone with an interest in land is obliged to pay under an EMS is an estate charge.

6.23   LVTs exercise similar control over estate charges as they do over administration charges. The only important difference in the treatment of estate charges is that there is no concept of a 'party to a lease' for an EMS. Anyone who has an obligation to pay any estate charge may apply for the variation of an EMS in respect of fixed estate charges. The applicant need not be obliged to pay the estate charge in respect of which he or she is applying for a variation.

6.24   The creation of EMSs, or their variation for reasons unconnected with estate charges, is properly considered as part of the process of enfranchisement and thus beyond the scope of this work, though LVTs do exercise jurisdiction. Estate management schemes are comparatively rare and it is not anticipated that any readers of this work will be affected by them.

---

15   CLRA 2002 Sch 11 para 4(3).
16   See generally Leasehold Reform Act 1967 s19, and Leasehold Reform, Housing and Urban Development Act 1993 Part 1 chapters 1 and 4 or section 94(6) in respect of the Crown.

Variation of leases

Key points

- Any party to a lease may apply to vary a lease. 'Right to manage' companies are treated as a party, but managing agents are not.
- An application may be made if the lease of a flat fails to make satisfactory provision for:
  - repair or maintenance of the building;
  - repair or maintenance of the installations;
  - insurance;
  - provision or maintenance of services;
  - recovery of expenditure;
  - computation of service charges.
- The lease of a house may only be varied if it fails to make satisfactory provision for the insurance of the house.
- It is possible to apply to have a number of leases, such as all those relating to a block of flats, to be varied at once. A qualified majority of tenants would be needed in these situations.
- A Leasehold Valuation Tribunal may order compensation to be paid to any person suffering loss or disadvantage as a result of the variation. The LVT must refuse to vary a lease where this would result in substantial prejudice to any person.
- The varied lease is binding on third parties and any successors in title.
- It is the duty of the applicant to inform the respondent and anyone else they know or have reason to believe may be affected by the variation. Failure to do so may result in the variation being set aside and the payment of damages to those affected.

Tips for advisers

- Proposed variations should be drafted by a legally qualified person in order to reduce the prospect of delay, re-drafting and amendment. An LVT will not accept a variation that will cause problems in the future.

Introduction

7.1   Many leases are, by any objective view, defective. For example the lease may not specify who is to pay for work that needs to be done or it may allocate service charges in a way that does not add up to 100 per cent of the total cost. These kinds of situation may arise because the lease was poorly drafted or because it was drafted before the development of modern property management. This chapter explains one remedy open to the parties to a lease: an application to an LVT for the variation of a lease.

7.2 Those responding to an application to vary a lease may make a related application to vary any other lease to which they are a party on the same grounds.

7.3 There is also a procedure whereby a group of tenants can apply to vary all the leases in respect of a property. The law on the variation of leases is contained in Landlord and Tenant Act (LTA) 1987 Part IV. Since 30 September 2003[1] Leasehold Valuation Tribunals has exclusive jurisdiction to deal with such matters.[2]

7.4 The powers of an LVT to vary a lease thus far described are restricted to leases of flats. There is an alternative procedure for the variation of the insurance provision of a leasehold house and this is the only power the LVT has to vary such a lease.

7.5 Unlike all other applications to an LVT it is the duty of the applicant to notify respondents and others who might be affected by the application. By contrast in all other applications described in this book, it is the duty of the LVT to notify respondents and others of any application.

Any person who should have been notified of an application to vary a lease, but was not, may apply to have the variation cancelled or modified, or sue the applicant(s) for damages.[3]

Application to vary an individual lease

Who may vary a lease?

7.6 Only a party to the lease may apply for its variation. A 'right to manage' company (see chapter 7) that has acquired the right to manage the property counts as a party to the lease for the purposes of this chapter[3a] but a managing agent – even one appointed by a court or tribunal – does not. The jurisdiction discussed in this chapter under which an LVT may vary a lease extends only to long leases which are:

* leases granted for more than 21 years;

1 Commonhold and Leasehold Reform Act 2002 (Commencement No 2 and Savings) (England) Order 2003 rule 2(a).
2 Commonhold and Leasehold Reform Act (CLRA) 2002 s163.
3 LTA 1987 s39(3).
3a CLRA 2002 Sch 7 para 10.

- leases granted with an obligation on the landlord to renew them perpetually[4] (unless they are subleases of short leases); or
- right to buy leases.

Grounds for varying a lease

7.7   There are a number of grounds on which an application for the variation of a lease may be made, all of which concern occasions in which the lease has failed to make satisfactory provision.[5] In general terms they are: repair or maintenance of the building, insurance, repair or maintenance of installations; provision or maintenance of services, recovery of expenditure and the computation of service charges.

Repair or maintenance

7.8   'Repair or maintenance' applies not only to the repair or maintenance of the flat itself[6] and the building in which it is contained[7] but of any other land or building which is let to the tenant or over which the tenant also has rights under the lease.[8]

7.9   Thus if the lease fails to provide for repair or maintenance to external garages, recreation areas or laundries an application to vary the lease could be made so as to make the landlord responsible for their upkeep, subject to the recovery of costs through the service charge bill.

Insurance

7.10   In the same way, 'insurance' applies to all such property which has been leased to a tenant or over which they have rights given by the lease.[9]

7.11   The power of the LVT to vary provisions of a lease concerning insurance is restricted in three ways. The LVT cannot vary a term of the lease which gives the landlord the right to nominate an insurer; nor may the LVT insert a term that requires the landlord to nominate a list of insurers from which the tenant would be entitled to select; nor

4   See Megarry and Wade *Law of Real Property* (Sweet & Maxwell, 6th edn, 1996) 14-089 and Law of Property Act 1925 s145.
5   Landlord and Tenant Act (LTA) 1987 s35(2).
6   LTA 1987 s35(2)(a)(i).
7   LTA 1987 s35(2)(a)(ii).
8   LTA 1987 s35(2)(a)(iii).
9   LTA 1987 s35(2)(b).

may the lease be varied so that it requires insurance with a particular insurer.[10]

7.12   Chapter 4 discusses other options a tenant might have if they are dissatisfied with their insurance. There is also a right for tenants of leasehold houses to challenge their insurance provisions (see para 7.33 below).

Repair or maintenance of any installations

7.13   'Repair or maintenance of any installations' applies to those which are reasonably necessary to ensure that occupiers of the flat enjoy a reasonable standard of accommodation.[11]

7.14   This includes factors relating to the common parts of the building containing the flat[12] as well as the safety and security of the flat, its occupiers and the common parts of that building[13] and so ought certainly to apply to door entry systems, for example.

7.15   It is less clear how far 'necessary' extends. Lighting of the common parts and lifts giving access to upper floors in high-rise flats would seem uncontroversial while provision of cable television is almost certainly not required for the enjoyment of a reasonable standard of accommodation.

Provision or maintenance of services

7.16   Exactly the same considerations as above apply to provision or maintenance of services,[14] so that cleaning of the common parts would certainly be included while the delivery of newspapers would almost certainly not.

Service charges

7.17   Provision for the computation of service charges payable under the lease includes the manner in which the amount payable for the failure to pay a service charge on time is determined[15] (such a payment would constitute an administration charge – see chapter 6).

7.18   A very common problem with poorly drafted leases is that the total service charge bill is apportioned between tenants (and sometimes

10   LTA 1987 s38(7).
11   LTA 1987 s35(2)(c).
12   LTA 1987 s35(3)(b).
13   LTA 1987 s35(3)(a).
14   LTA 1987 s35(2)(d).
15   LTA 1987 s35(3A).

the landlord) in proportions that do not add up to 100 per cent. The result is either the landlord suffers due to a shortfall or the tenants collectively pay more than their fair share. This problem is explicitly included under the heading 'failure to properly provide for the calculation of service charges'.[16]

Application to vary other leases

7.19　Once an application to vary a lease (the original lease) has been made, any other party to the lease may apply to an LVT asking it to vary other leases if an order is made varying the original lease. The other leases must share the same landlord as the original lease,[17] though they need not be leases for flats in the same building.

7.20　For example where a tenant applies for the variation of their lease, a respondent landlord may wish to use the opportunity to vary all their other leases in the same or a similar way. The grounds for this supplementary application must be the same as the original application. So if, for example, a respondent landlord wished to make various additional variations then a fresh application would be needed.

7.21　It must also be shown that it would be in the respondent's interest or in the interests of the other parties to the various leases to have them varied to the same effect.[18] Such applications are likely to be restricted to landlords since it is unlikely that a tenant would be a party to multiple leases from the same landlord.

Application by a majority

7.22　In cases where one lease is defective it will be very common for most or all the other leases of flats from the landlord also to be defective. In such a case an application for variation of some or all of the relevant leases may be made if, as defined below, a sufficient proportion of the parties to the lease agree.

7.23　Such an application may be made by the landlord or any of the tenants under the lease.[19] An application may only be made in respect of

---

16　LTA 1987 s35(4).
17　LTA 1987 s36(2).
18　LTA 1987 s36(3).
19　LTA 1987 s37(4).

two or more leases. All the leases must be made with the same land-lord though they need not all be in the same building nor need the leases be in identical terms.[20]

7.24 An application may only be made if it is supported by a minimum number of parties to the various leases involved. Where someone is a party to more than one lease he or she counts as more than one party.[21] Joint tenants of a lease count as one party.

7.25 Where there are fewer than 9 dwellings then all, or all but one, of the parties must agree.[22] Where there are 9 or more dwellings, at least 75 per cent of the parties must consent and no more than 10 per cent may oppose the application.[23]

7.26 Such an application may only be made if the object to be achieved by the variation cannot be satisfactorily achieved unless all the leases are varied to the same effect.[24] From this it would appear that an application of this kind is not restricted to the grounds listed at para 7.7 above, though the restrictions on the kind of variation an LVT can make to the insurance provisions of a lease (see para 7.11) will still apply.

Orders varying a lease

7.27 If an LVT is satisfied that the grounds for an application for the variation of a lease have been made out then they may make an order varying the lease.[25] Though the LVT will normally make an order for a variation in accordance with that submitted by the applicant(s) they have the power to make any variation they think fit.[26] Applicant(s) cannot restrict the LVT to either accepting or rejecting the variation they have put forward. The LVT only has the power to vary those leases for which the grounds for application have been made out.[27] Such an order may directly vary the lease or it may direct the parties to carry out the variation.[28]

---

20 LTA 1987 s37(2).
21 LTA 1987 s37(6)(a).
22 LTA 1987 s37(5)(a).
23 LTA 1987 s37(5)(b).
24 LTA 1987 s37(3).
25 LTA 1987 s38(1).
26 LTA 1987 s38(4).
27 LTA 1987 s38(5).
28 LTA 1987 s38(8).

7.28   In order to reduce the prospect of delay, re-drafting and amendment, it is suggested that any proposed variations be drafted by a
legally qualified person. An LVT is likely to scrutinise the wording
and terminology of the proposed variation with some care and non-
lawyers may not appreciate the full effect of the proposed variation. In
particular, two important checks should be carried out in respect of
any proposed variation:

a) if the proposed variation introduces a new term, that term must be
adequately defined;

b) the proposed variation must take into account any changes which
will be necessitated to the rest of the lease. Although a lease contains many schedules and sections, it must be read and, after the
proposed variation, must be able to continue to be read as a con-
tinuous and internally coherent document.

7.29   The LVT's power to vary a lease is moderated in two respects. Firstly
there is a power to order that any party to the lease pay any other person (not necessarily a party to the lease) compensation for any loss or
disadvantage they are likely to suffer as a result of the variation.[29]

7.30   Secondly, if there would be substantial prejudice to any person
and where an order for payment would not be adequate compensation the LVT must not order a variation. The LVT may also refuse to
make an order if for any other reason 'it would not be reasonable in
the circumstances.'[30]

7.31   An order for the variation of a lease is binding on third parties and
is not restricted to those who were parties to the lease at the time of
the application.[31] In particular it is binding on any surety who guar-
anteed the performance (whether by a tenant or landlord) of any obligation under the lease despite the fact that the obligation may be
changed by the variation.[32]

7.32   Anyone who should have been notified of the application to the
LVT by the applicant, but who was not notified, may apply to the LVT
for the cancellation or modification of the variation.[33] The LVT may
either accede to their request or order the payment of compensation.[34]
If the LVT cancels or modifies the variation it may backdate that can-

29   LTA 1987 s38(10).
30   LTA 1987 s38(6).
31   LTA 1987 s39(1).
32   LTA 1987 s39(2).
33   LTA 1987 s39(3).
34   LTA 1987 s39(4).

cellation or modification so that it takes effect on the date the original variation was ordered or it may order it to take effect on any later date that it sees fit.[35]

Insurance of dwellings houses

7.33　An application to vary the lease of a dwelling that is not a flat may also be made, but only on the ground that the lease fails to make satisfactory provision with respect to insurance, including the recovery of the costs of such insurance.[36] The power of the LVT to make an order for variation in respect of insurance provisions is restricted in the same way as for long leases of flats (see para 7.11).

7.34　Such an application may only be made by a tenant who holds long leases in respect of two or fewer dwellings from the same landlord.[37] Where the tenant is a company this includes leases held by associated companies.[38] There is no corresponding right for a respondent to apply for the variation of additional leases or for a majority of leaseholders of the same landlord to make an application for variation of a lease.

35　LTA 1987 s39(5).
36　LTA 1987 s40(1).
37　LTA 1987 s40(4A).
38　LTA 1987 s40(4B).

Appointment of a manager

Key points

- A common complaint of tenants is that their property has been badly managed. Many service charge disputes have poor property management as their cause. The Leasehold Valuation Tribunal (LVT) has a power to appoint a manager where problems arise.
- There are a number of limits on the right to apply to an LVT. The most important is that 'resident landlords' who live in the property and manage it themselves are usually exempt from having applications made against them.
- The LVT regards the appointment of a manager against the wishes of the landlord to be a draconian step and will usually require certain preliminary stages to be completed. In exceptional circumstances, an LVT will be willing to waive compliance.
- A tenant must show that it would be just and convenient in all the circumstances for a manager to be appointed.
- The tenant must also show one of the following:
  - one of the respondents is in breach of a management obligation under the lease;
  - unreasonable service charge demands have been made, are proposed or are likely to be made;
  - unreasonable variable administration charge demands have been made, are proposed or are likely to be made;
  - there have been breaches of the relevant codes of practice;
  - other circumstances exist which make it just and convenient for the order to be made.

Tips for advisers

- There is no requirement that a professional manager be appointed but LVTs prefer this to be the case.

Introduction

8.1   The property manager is becoming more common, in particular as institutional and commercial landlords seek to appoint professional companies to discharge their obligations under the lease. The mere fact that a company or individual holds itself out as a professional manager is no guarantee of quality and situations frequently arise where tenants are dissatisfied with the management of the property, either by their landlord or a manager appointed by the landlord or by a 'right to manage' manager (discussed in chapter 9).

8.2   To deal with these problems, the LVT has the power to appoint a manager or receiver (or both functions vested in one person)[1] and where the LVT has jurisdiction its jurisdiction is exclusive.[2]

What is management?

8.3   The term management is not defined but includes repair, maintenance, improvements and insurance of any premises.[3]

Who may apply?

8.4   LVTs have jurisdiction to appoint a manager or receiver, provided that the following conditions are met:

a) the property consists of two or more flats;[4]
b) the landlord is not an 'exempt landlord';
c) the landlord is not a 'residential landlord' (except where at least half the flats in the premises are held on long leases);
d) the premises are not included within the functional land of a charity;[5]
e) the tenancy is not a business tenancy to which Landlord and Tenant Act 1954 Part II applies[6] (although such a tenant could apply to the court under its general jurisdiction to appoint a receiver or manager);[7]
f) the property is not subject to a Crown Interest.[8]

1   Landlord and Tenant Act (LTA) 1987 s24(1).
2   *Stylli v Haberton Properties Ltd* [2002] EWHC 394. See also LTA 1987 s21(6).
3   LTA 1987 s21(11).
4   LTA 1987 s21(2).
5   LTA 1987 s21(3)(b).
6   LTA 1987 s21(5).
7   Supreme Court Act 1981 s37(1).
8   LTA 1987 s56.

Exempt landlords

8.5   A tenant whose landlord is any of the following bodies is not permitted to bring an application to an LVT:[9]

- A local authority or joint authority;
- The Commissioner for New Towns or a Development Corporation;
- An Urban Development Corporation;
- A Housing Action Trust;
- The Broads Authority;
- A National Park Authority;
- The Housing Corporation;
- A charitable housing trust;
- A registered housing association or a fully mutual housing association;
- A joint waste disposal authority.[10]

Resident landlords

8.6   A certain amount of protection is given to landlords who actually live in the property who, it might be assumed, have a greater interest in its management. A landlord is a 'resident landlord' if:

a) the property in question is not and does not form a purpose-built block of flats; and

b) the landlord occupies a flat contained in the premises as his only or principal residence; and

c) has done so for a period of at least 12 months.[11]

8.7   However, the resident landlord exception does not apply where at least half the flats contained in the premises are held on relevant long leases.[12] It would appear that a landlord who divides his or her house into two and leases the other half on a long lease would be subject to an LVT's jurisdiction.

---

9   LTA 1987 s21(3).
10   LTA 1987 s58(1).
11   LTA 1987 s58(2).
12   LTA 1987 s21(3A).

Pre-application procedure

8.8 Provided an LVT has jurisdiction, a single tenant, or several tenants jointly, may apply to the LVT for the appointment of a manager. The tenant(s) must complete a relatively lengthy pre-application procedure before bringing the application. Though it is possible for an LVT to make an order dispensing with the notice requirements every effort should be made to comply with them since the LVT regards the appointment of a manager as a last resort.

8.9 The first step is for the tenant to give a 'preliminary notice'[13] to the landlord and to any other person who has management duties under the lease. A manager whose duties are not due under the lease, for example a managing agent, does not need to be served with the notice. The notice must set out:

a) the name and address of the flat and the name and address where notices can be served on the tenant if different from the address of the flat;

b) a statement that the tenant intends to make an application for an order that a manager be appointed;

c) the grounds on which the tenant will ask the LVT to make the order and the matters that will be relied on by the tenant as evidence of the grounds;

d) where the matters of which the tenant is complaining can be remedied by the landlord or other manager, a statement requiring the landlord or manager to remedy the problems set out and giving a reasonable period for this to take place.

e) any other information as may be specified under regulations made by the secretary of state.[14]

If the notice is sent by post, it should be sent by recorded delivery.

8.10 If there is a mortgage on the property the landlord must serve on the mortgagee a copy of the notice as soon as practicable.[15]

8.11 The 'reasonable period' for remedying the problems will depend on the circumstances of each case. The more substantial the complaint, the longer will be needed to remedy it. As a general rule however, 14 days should be considered the absolute minimum 'reasonable period' that the tenant should offer.

---

13 LTA 1987 s22.
14 No such regulations have been made at time of writing.
15 LTA 1987 s22(4).

8.12   If, at the conclusion of the 'reasonable period' the tenant remains dissatisfied, the application to the LVT should proceed.

Dispensation if service is impracticable

8.13   If it is not considered reasonably practicable[16] to serve the notice, the LVT may grant a dispensation. If problems with properly serving the notices (for example, where the landlord cannot be found) are anticipated in advance, a free-standing application can be made to the LVT to make such a dispensation. On the other hand where problems with the service of notice only become apparent at a late stage, the application can be considered at the hearing of the application for an order appointing a manager itself. If an LVT does grant such dispensation it may direct the tenants to take some other appropriate steps in an attempt to notify the landlord before allowing the application to continue.

8.14   Tenants should not rely on the LVT granting dispensation as a matter of course and they will be expected to produce evidence of the impracticability of serving the notice. Evidence that the Post Office were unable to deliver the documents should be sufficient.

8.15   If an LVT is not satisfied that the requirements of LTA 1987 s22 were complied with, it may refuse to hear the application. The tenants would then have to start the process over again and complete the pre-application process correctly.

Grounds for application

8.16   In order to exercise its powers of appointment, the LVT must be convinced both that it would be just and convenient in all the circumstances to do so and:

a) that the person complained about is in breach of an obligation under the lease relating to the management of the property;[17] or
b) that unreasonable service charges have been made, are proposed or are likely to be made;[18] or
c) that unreasonable variable administration charges have been made, or are proposed or likely to be made;[19] or

16   LTA1985 s22(3).
17   LTA 1987 s24(2)(a).
18   LTA 1987 s24(2)(ab).
19   LTA 1987 s24(2)(aba).

d) that there have been breaches of the relevant codes of practice[20] made under Leasehold Reform, Housing and Urban Development Act 1993 s87.[21]

8.17 Alternatively, the LVT possesses a power to make an order if other, undefined circumstances exist which make it just and convenient for the order to be made.[22]

8.18 Most applications which fail do so because they fail to meet the 'just and convenient' test. The tribunal is likely to be impressed with attempts by the applicant to assist the landlord in remedying any problems and any efforts made to negotiate a settlement and avoid the need for the imposition of a manager on an unwilling landlord.

8.19 The remaining grounds are relatively self-explanatory. Service charges and variable administration charges are given the same interpretation as those used elsewhere in this work (at paras 2.4 and 6.3, for example).[23]

8.20 One point to note is that a service charge need not be determined as unreasonable under an LTA 185 s27A application, although such a determination would provide highly compelling evidence. In this context 'unreasonable' includes the following situations:[24]

- the amount charged is unreasonable having regard to the items for which it is payable;
- the items for which it is payable are of an unnecessarily high standard; or
- the items for which it is payable are of an insufficient standard such that additional service charges may be or have been incurred.

8.21 In reality, the LVT are loath to make an order if only ground (d) at para 8.16 can be made out. Unreasonable financial demands or breaches of obligations under the lease carry more weight and tenants should emphasise any such factors in their application.

8.22 Any application to the LVT must include a copy of the preliminary notice that was served on the landlord.

---

20 There are currently two, one produced by the Association of Retirement Housing Managers and one by the Royal Institute of Chartered Surveyors. Copies of the codes are available directly from these bodies and contact details are given in appendix A.

21 LTA 1987 s24(2)(ac).

22 LTA 1987 s24(2)(b).

23 LTA 1987 s24(2A)(c) and (2B).

24 LTA 1987 s24(2A).

Who can be a manager?

8.23   There is no requirement that an LVT appoint a professional manager and tenants are frequently known to suggest that one of their own number be appointed. However, the LVT is often sceptical of such suggestions, and informally presumes it would not be just and convenient to make such an order, fearing that this would not resolve the dispute. Tenants are strongly advised to suggest one or more possible managers and to select them from professional management companies.

8.24   One of the most common grounds for rejecting a proposed manager is a deemed lack of experience – a problem which clearly should not arise in the case of professional management companies. Professional companies should also have adequate professional indemnity insurance, another factor known to impress LVTs.

8.25   When deciding who to nominate as a manager, tenants should be aware that the LVT will usually make management orders for two to three years, with longer terms being exceptional, and a shorter term even more exceptional.[25] It is vital that, as far as possible, all tenants, not just those bringing the application, support the suggested manager. LVTs regard the decision to 'strip the landlord of his right to maintain his own building' as 'draconian' and not to be invoked lightly.[26] If there are tenants who are not parties to the application, they should be asked to provide letters of support for the proposed manager suggested by the applicants.

Form of any order made

8.26   Any order made by an LVT may make provision for:[27]

a) matters relating to the exercise of the management functions prescribed under the order; and

b) any incidental or ancillary matters as the LVT thinks fit. There is a residual right for the manager to apply to the LVT for directions.

8.27   In particular, an order may provide for:

a) the rights and liabilities of contracts to which the manager is not a party being transferred to the manager;

25   *Re 60–62 Palace Road, London* LVT/SC/08/041&042/03.

26   *Re 26 and 28 Birdhurst Rise, South Croydon* LON/00AH/NAM/2003/006.

27   LTA 1987 s24(4).

b) the right of a manager to prosecute causes of action accruing before or after the date of his appointment;
c) remuneration to be paid to the manager;
d) for the managers functions to be time limited.

8.28 The order may have any conditions the LVT thinks fit added to it, including the suspension of the order on terms fixed by the LVT.

Miscellaneous

8.29 Any manager appointed by an LVT does not step into the shoes of the landlord. This means, among other things, that a tenant cannot set off against a manager's claim for service charges damages claimed against a landlord for breach of a duty to repair.[28]

Variation or discharge of any order made

8.30 An order may only be discharged or varied if an LVT is satisfied that to do so would not cause the initial problem to recur and it is just and convenient to do so.[29] A mere change in the circumstances of the property does not discharge the order.[30]

8.31 In the unlikely event that the manager with whom a party is dissatisfied was himself appointed by an LVT, an application[31] should be made to vary or discharge the existing order, rather than as a new application for the appointment of a manager.

8.32 This is also the correct procedure where a manager appointed by the tribunal resigns[32] or if the appointed manager wishes to have their term extended. An extension of a term does not need to be for a reason set out in LTA 1987 s24(2) but is a free standing power of LVTs.[33]

---

28 *Maurice Taylor v Blaquiere* [2002] EWCA Civ 1633; [2003] 1 WLR 379; [2003] 1 EGLR 52.
29 LTA 1987 s24(9A).
30 LTA 1987 s24(10).
31 LTA 1987 s24(4)(9).
32 See *Re 168 Grenville Road, Plymouth* CHI/00HG/NMV/2003.
33 *Orchard Court Residents Association v St Anthony Homes Ltd* [2003] EWCA Civ 1049; (2003) 33 EG 64.

Consultation about managing agents

8.33   Recognised tenants' associations have the right to be consulted about managing agents.[34] The association may, at any time, serve a notice on the landlord requesting him to consult the association in relation to the appointment or employment of a managing agent. If such an agent is employed, the landlord must, within a month, serve a notice on the association specifying the obligations which the manager discharges on the landlord's behalf and allowing a reasonable period for the association to comment on the manner in which the managing agent has been discharging the obligations and the desirability of this continuing.[35]

8.34   If no such agent is employed when the notice is served, the landlord must, before employing any managing agent at any future stage, serve a notice setting out the name of the proposed managing agent, the obligations he proposes to have the agent discharge and allowing a period of at least one month for the association to make observations on the appointment.[36]

8.35   Once the initial notice has been served, the landlord must, at least once every five years, serve on the association a notice specifying any changes which have occurred since the date of the last notice served on him by the association and allow the association a reasonable period to comment on the manner in which the managing agent has discharged his obligations and the desirability of him continuing to do so.[37]

8.36   He must also serve on the association the name and proposed duties of any new managing agent and allow a period of not less than one month for comments.[38]

8.37   The residents association may release the landlord from these obligations at any stage by serving a notice on him to this effect.[39] Any consultation obligations cease if the property becomes vested in a new landlord, although they may be reasserted in the manner set out above.[40]

34 LTA 1985 s30B.
35 LTA 1985 s30B(1).
36 LTA 1985 s30B(2).
37 LTA 1985 s30B(4).
38 LTA 1985 s30B(4)(b).
39 LTA 1985 s30B(5).
40 LTA 1985 s30B(6).

Right to manage companies

continued

Key points

- CLRA 2002 created a 'no fault' right to manage. Leaseholders can now establish a Right to Manage (RTM) company. This is not a simple procedure and a legal adviser should be consulted.
- The first step is to establish an RTM company, which all 'qualifying tenants' are entitled to join.
- The RTM company may then obtain various information from the landlord to decide whether or not to continue the process.
- Before the right to manage can be acquired all qualifying tenants must be invited to join the company and at least half must be members. After this a notice of the company's intention to take control of the management of the property must be served on the landlord and tenants.
- At this stage anyone objecting may serve a counter notice, alleging for example that the RTM company was not validly formed. An LVT may then be required to adjudicate between the parties.
- If the disputes are resolved in the RTM company's favour, it will acquire the right to manage the property.
- The right to manage does not apply to all properties and cannot be established against all landlords. Most local authority tenancies, for example, are exempt.

Tips for advisers

- RTM companies are hard work and legal advice will almost always be needed. Those who establish the company are usually liable for the costs associated with the process, including the landlords costs.
- In addition, an RTM company would place tenants in the position of having to collect service charges from each other. This may mean that relationships are strained. There may be a tension between the duties of the RTM company and its directors, and the desires of friends and other tenants.

Introduction

9.1   The Commonhold and Leasehold Reform Act (CLRA) 2002[1] creates a new 'no fault' right to manage on the part of the leaseholders who can now force the landlord to transfer the management functions to a

---

1   Chapter 1, Part 2.

special kind of company, called a Right to Manage (RTM) company. There is no need for the landlord to consent to the establishment of an RTM company and no order of a court or LVT is necessary. The right is available regardless of any alleged deficiencies in the existing management.

Stages of the RTM process

9.2   The acquisition of the right to manage begins with the creation of an RTM company. As soon as it is created 'qualifying tenants' are entitled to join it. An RTM company has the right to obtain various pieces of information from the freeholder and others in order to take the next steps in the process.

9.3   The RTM company may then inform qualifying tenants of its intention to take over the management of the building and invite them to join by sending a 'notice of intention'. Once the RTM company has sent a 'notice of intention' and more than half of the qualifying tenants have become members of the company it may then serve a 'notice of claim', this time on all parties to the various leases of the flats.

9.4   Anybody objecting to the RTM company's right to acquire the right to manage (for example, because it was not validly formed) may serve a 'counter notice'. An LVT will resolve any disputes raised in a counter notice.

9.5   Once the time limit specified in a claim notice has expired and all disputes have been properly resolved, the RTM company will take over the management functions of the building.

Properties to which RTM applies

The building

9.6   The right to manage is always exercised in relation to particular premises. The premises must be either a self-contained building or a 'part' of a building together with any appurtenant property.[2] There does not seem to be anything to stop an RTM company being formed in respect of several premises, something that is commonly done with tenants' associations, but the process of acquiring the right to manage is exercised separately in respect of each premises.

2   CLRA 2002 s72(1)(a).

9.7 A self-contained building is one which is structurally detached.[3] A 'part' of a building must also:

a) have a vertical division of the building, which is likely to be defeated if there is a small overlap with another 'part' of the building;[4]

b) be capable of being redeveloped independently of the rest of the building;[5]

c) have 'relevant services', which are provided independently from the rest of the building, or could be so provided without significantly interrupting the supply of those services to the rest of the building.[6]

9.8 The sort of situation avoided by the last condition would be a part of a building whose water supply was so intertwined with the rest of the building that it would be impractical to separate it out. The key goal of these rules seems to be that the RTM company should deal only with a coherent manageable unit.

Tenants

9.9 There must be at least two qualifying tenants in the premises (see para 9.18 above) and at least two-thirds of the flats must be held by qualifying tenants.[7]

Non-residential use

9.10 The premises do not have to be entirely residential. Up to 25 per cent of the internal floor area of the premises may be in non-residential use. For the purposes of calculating the floor area and the percentage in non-residential use, the common parts are disregarded.[8]

Landlords

9.11 It does not matter if the premises are owned by more than one free-holder but where a freeholder owns a part of a building which would

---

3   CLRA 2002 s72(2).
4   *Malekshad v Howard de Walden Estates (No 1)* [2002] UKHL 49; [2003] 1 AC 1013.
5   CLRA 2002 s72(3)(b).
6   CLRA 2002 s72(4).
7   CLRA 2002 s72(1).
8   CLRA 2002 Sch 6 para 1.

be a self-contained part, the right to manage would have to be exercised for that part independently.[9]

9.12   An RTM company cannot be established where a local housing authority is the immediate landlord of any of the qualifying tenants. This is true, regardless of how many other qualifying tenants there are in the premises or the identity of the freeholder.[10] The thinking seems to be that tenants of a local housing authority have the right to set up what is called a Tenant Management Organisation (TMO), which is better suited to public-sector tenants. In fact a TMO may not always be a possible alternative. There is considerable guidance on the formation and management of TMOs on the National Federation of Tenant Management Organisation's website[11] as well as at the website of the Office of the Deputy Prime Minister.[12]

9.13   The right to manage applies to all other social and private sector landlords even those with a Crown interest.[13]

Resident landlords

9.14   There is a further exception for situations where there is a resident landlord.[14] The exception is a narrow one and requires that:

a) there are four or fewer units in the premises;

b) the premises are not a purpose-built block of flats; and

c) the landlord, or a member of the landlord's family occupies one of the qualifying flats as their only or principal home.

9.15   The residential occupation must either have been for at least the previous 12 months;[15] or if the freeholder has more recently acquired the freehold, the occupation must have started within 28 days of the acquisition and been maintained since then.[16]

9.16   A member of the landlord's family is restricted to parents and children and children-in-law of the landlord or the landlord's spouse. The relationship must be by blood or marriage, so that children or parents of a long term partner or civil partner would be excluded.

---

9   CLRA 2002 Sch 6 para 2.

10   CLRA 2002 Sch 6 para 4.

11   www.tmonatfed.com/information.html

12   www.odpm.gov.uk/stellent/groups/odpm_control/documents/
contentservertemplate/odpm_index.

13   CLRA 2002 s108.

14   CLRA 2002 Sch 6 para 3

15   CLRA 2002 Sch 6 para 3(4).

16   CLRA 2002 Sch 6 para 3(5).

Here the legislation takes a distinctly less modern approach than that for entitlement to waiver of fees where 'spouse' is construed very broadly and a more liberal interpretation may be read into it as a result of the decision of the House of Lords in *Fitzpatrick v Stirling Housing Association*[17] and *Ghaidan v Godin-Mendoza*.[18]

Previous RTM companies

9.17 Where the right to manage has been exercisable by an RTM company within the previous four years and has ceased to be exercisable then any further attempt to acquire the right is prohibited.[19] An application can be made to an LVT to ask that the prohibition be lifted; the LVT will lift the restriction if it would be unreasonable for it to apply in the circumstances of the case.[20]

Qualifying tenants

9.18 A qualifying tenant is someone who is a tenant of a flat under a long lease,[21] which is not a business tenancy; or a lease granted out of another lease, which itself was not a long lease, and where that grant was made in unwaived breach of the superior lease. No flat has more than one qualifying tenant and joint tenants are regarded jointly as the qualifying tenant.

9.19 A long lease is, for these purposes:[22]

- granted for a term exceeding 21 years;
- granted for a term fixed by law with a covenant or obligation for perpetual renewal;
- one which took effect under Law of Property Act 1925 s149(6) (that is a lease for life);
- granted in pursuance of the right to buy under Housing Act 1985 Part V;
- a shared ownership lease where the tenants' share is 100 per cent; or
- granted pursuant to of the Housing Act 1996 s17.

9.20 There is no requirement that the 'qualifying tenant' actually be resident in the property, nor that they only own one flat within the property.

17 [2001] 1 AC 27.
18 [2004] UKHL 30.
19 CLRA 2002 Sch 6 para 5(1)(b).
20 CLRA 2002 Sch 6 para 5(3).
21 CLRA 2002 s75.
22 CLRA 2002 s76.

Preparation

9.21   The establishment of an RTM company is not something to be undertaken lightly and before attempting to do so, tenants should understand what they will be taking on as well as being very clear about what they want to achieve.

9.22   The advantage of an RTM company is that it allows long lease-holders much greater control of their property. Where a landlord has been unwilling or incapable of managing the property or appointing an agent to do so, the right to manage has the advantage of being much more certain than the appointment of a manager by a court or LVT. Even where a landlord has not managed the property badly, tenants may prefer to make the management decisions themselves rather than leaving them to a landlord who may have little stake in the property.

9.23   There are distinct dangers with creating an RTM company which must also carefully be considered. Depending on the size and complexity of the property, the process may be costly and most of that cost will be borne by the promoters of the company. The company will also take over many of the duties and responsibilities of the landlord.

9.24   The hardest aspect of running an RTM company is that in order to pay for management it will have to collect service charges from tenants. This could place directors in conflict with their friends and neighbours if disputes about service charge demands arise. There will inevitably be a tension between the duties of the RTM company to ensure adequate and prompt repairs and maintenance, and the desires of the tenants to keep costs down.

9.25   There is also a difficulty with continuity of management, especially where there are a relatively small number of members of the RTM company. The moment a tenant sells their flat, they cease to be a member of the company. This means that even if the RTM starts with an enthusiastic group prepared to run it well, that group will change over the years and the RTM may run into problems.

9.26   Independent professional advice will almost always be necessary. It may be that the RTM company will need to employ lawyers and accountants in order to meet its legal obligations.

9.27   The RTM company represents a considerable investment in terms of time and energy on the part of the tenants and the benefits may not be entirely obvious. If the tenants' objectives can be achieved without establishing an RTM company, it is almost certainly preferable to do so.

Creating the RTM company

9.28   The first step in the acquisition of the right to manage is the creation of an RTM company in respect of the premises. A company either is, or is not, an RTM company in respect of particular premises.

9.29   A company which is not also a commonhold association[23] and which:[24]

a) is limited by guarantee; and
b) has the acquisition and exercise of the right to manage certain premises as one of its objects in the memorandum of association;

is an RTM company in respect of those premises, subject to a number of exceptions.

A pre-existing RTM company

9.30   If there is already an RTM company in respect of those premises or any premises containing, or contained in those premises then the second company created is not the RTM company in respect of those premises: the earlier company takes priority.[25]

9.31   This has very unsatisfactory consequences. The first is that nobody needs to be informed of the existence of an RTM company. An anti-social tenant or landlord could keep the existence of an earlier RTM company hidden until the service of a notice of claim[26] by the later RTM company. Then the owner of the earlier RTM company could derail the RTM process by a counter-notice. Since the creator of an RTM company need not have any interest in the premises in question there is considerable scope for trouble to be caused by unscrupulous persons.

9.32   Of course it is open to all qualifying tenants to join the pre-existing company and exercise the right to manage from it.

9.33   The second difficulty is where buildings consist of several parts, tenants may have different views as to whether they wish the building to be managed as a whole or in its separate parts. Whoever 'gets in first' by creating an RTM company can determine the structure of the future management of the building. There is no obvious legal remedy for anyone finding themselves in this situation.

---

23   CLRA 2002 s73(3).
24   CLRA 2002 s73.
25   CLRA 2002 s73(4).
26   See para 9.49 below.

Ownership of the building

9.34   If an RTM company comes to own the freehold of the premises, it ceases to be the RTM company in respect of those premises. The right to manage is not seen as consistent with ownership of the property.[27]

Setting up the RTM company

9.35   There are many firms that offer specialised RTM company creation services. Companies House also publishes a number of useful leaflets on creating and managing companies in general.

9.36   In order to create the company a number of 'promoters', who need not be qualifying tenants, must sign a memorandum of association (which sets out the company's objectives) and lodge it with the company's articles of association (its constitution) at Companies House.

9.37   Standard forms for the memorandum and articles of association are prescribed by statutory instrument.[28] Any part of the RTM company's memorandum and articles which conflict with those prescribed are void. One practical effect of this is that the company must have a name ending in 'RTM Company Ltd'.

9.38   Once the company is created, any qualifying tenant has the right to become a member (shareholder). Those promoters who were not qualifying tenants will cease to be members.

9.39   As a minimum a company needs a director and a secretary (who must be different people). In general it would be wise to start the company with more directors than this.

Obtaining information

9.40   As part of the process of planning the acquisition of the right to manage, an RTM company will need information of various kinds in order, for example, to put together the notice of claim. It will also usually want to begin the process of seeking out suitable companies with which to make management contracts. Some of this information can be obtained from public sources, but the RTM company also has a right to additional information.

9.41   An RTM company may, in respect of the premises for which it is an RTM company, give any person a notice requiring him or her to

27   CLRA s73(5).
28   SI 2120/2003.

provide any information which is in his or her possession or control and which the company reasonably requires for preparing any claim notice (see para 9.49 below).[29] Where the information is recorded in documentary form, the RTM company may require the holder to allow inspection of the document and to obtain copies.[30]

9.42   The person served with such a notice has 28 days from the day on which the notice is given to comply. A county court may make an order requiring compliance with a notice.[31]

Notice inviting participation[32]

9.43   The next stage on the way to acquiring the right to manage is to invite all qualifying tenants who have not agreed to become or are not currently members of the RTM company to become members. No one may be excluded for any reason.

9.44   The notice must be in writing and in the prescribed form[33] and must:[34]

a) state that the RTM company intends to acquire the right to manage;

b) state the names of the members of the RTM company;

c) invite the recipient to become a member of the RTM company;

d) include such other information as required by the regulations, currently:

- the RTM company's registered number and the address of its registered office;
- the names of its directors and secretary;
- the name of the landlord, plus the name of any other person who is a party to the lease other than the leaseholder;
- a statement that the RTM company will be responsible for the discharge of the landlord's duties under the lease and the exercise of his or her powers under the lease with respect to services, repairs, maintenance, improvements, insurance and management;

29 CLRA 2002 s82(1).
30 CLRA 2002 s82(2).
31 CLRA 2002 s107.
32 CLRA 2002 s78.
33 Right to Manage (Prescribed Particulars and Forms)(England) Regulations 2003 SI No 1988.
34 CLRA 2002 s78.

- a statement that the RTM may enforce untransferred tenant covenants;
- a statement that the RTM will not be responsible for the discharge of the landlord's duties or the exercise of his powers in relation to any matter concerning only a part of the premises not subject to a lease held by a qualifying tenant or relating to re-entry or forfeiture;
- a statement that the RTM company will have functions set out at CLRA 2002 Sch 7;
- a statement as to whether the RTM company intends to appoint a managing agent and, if so, the name of the proposed managing agent and whether or not that person was the landlord's managing agent. If no such appointment is intended, the qualifications and experience of members of the RTM company relating to management of residential property;
- a statement that the members of the RTM may be liable for the costs incurred by the landlord or others as a consequence of commencing the RTM process;
- a statement that, if the recipient of the notice does not fully understand it, he should seek professional (legal) assistance;
- a copy of the notes provided at Right to Manage (Prescribed Particulars and Forms)(England) Regulations 2003 Sch 1.

9.45   The notice must also be accompanied by a copy of the Memorandum of Association and Articles of Association or include a statement about the inspection and copying of the same documents.[35]

9.46   Despite these onerous requirements, a Notice Inviting Participation is not invalidated by any inaccuracy in the particulars required.[36] The legislative intent underlying the Notice Inviting Participation is clearly that leaseholders should have the opportunity to take part in the exercise of the RTM. Any procedural flaw will likely be deemed fatal only if it prevents this from taking place and, for example, a misspelling in the name of one Director would be far less serious than a failure to allow the inspection of the Articles and Memorandum of Association.

9.47   All those qualifying tenants who respond to the Notice and request membership must be enrolled as members of the RTM company[37] and their membership noted in the official records.

9.48   Although the legislation does not require the RTM company to

35 CLRA 2002 s78(4) and (5).
36 CLRA 2002 s78(7).
37 CLRA 2002 s74(1).

produce any form of plan or budget, it may be wise to do so as it will both focus the minds of those involved in the RTM process and provide clear direction for the RTM company. It may also forestall any objections from leaseholders or even the landlord about the costs and standards envisaged by the RTM.

Notice of claim

9.49 At least 14 days must be allowed to elapse after the notice of participation before the service of a notice of claim.[38] At least half of all qualifying tenants must also be members of the RTM company.[39]

9.50 The claim notice must be given to each person who, on the date at which the first notice of claim is served, is:[40]

a) a landlord under a lease of the whole or any part of the premises;
b) any other party to any such lease;
c) any manager appointed under the LTA 1987 procedure (see chapter 8). In this case a copy must also be sent to the LVT or court which appointed the manager;
d) a qualifying tenant of a flat contained in the premises.

9.51 There is no need to serve a claim notice on a person who cannot be found or whose identity cannot be ascertained. In this case an application should be made to the LVT[41] who will determine what, if any, further steps should be taken by the RTM company.

Contents of notice of claim

9.52 The notice of claim must be in writing and must:[42]

a) specify the premises and contain a statement listing all the criteria for qualification for RTM and that the property meets these;
b) state the full names and addresses of all those who are both qualifying tenants and members of the RTM company;
c) give sufficient summary information of each lease of each of these persons, including the date on which it was entered into, the term for which it was granted and the commencement of the term;
d) identify the registered office and name of the RTM company;

38 CLRA 2002 s79(2).
39 CLRA 2002 s79(5).
40 CLRA 2002 s79(6).
41 CLRA 2002 s85.
42 CLRA 2002 s80.

e) specify a date, not earlier than one month after the date of service of the notice of claim by which any counter notice is to be served;

f) specify a date, at least three months after the last date for counter notices to be served on which the RTM company intends to acquire the right to manage;

g) provide a statement informing the landlord that he or she may alert the RTM company to any inaccuracies in the notice (errors will not invalidate the notice);[43]

h) contain a reminder to the landlord, if they have no objection to the claim, to serve the relevant notices on those who have contracts (such as ontracts to undertake repairs) in respect of the property;

i) contain a statement that the landlord has a right to membership of the RTM company.

9.53   The notice of claim should be registered at the Land Registry, so that, even if the landlord sells the property before the RTM process is completed, the new purchaser will take the freehold subject to the notice.

Right of inspection

9.54   After a claim notice is served, those authorised by the RTM, the landlord, any other party to a lease or a manager must, upon giving ten days' written notice to any person occupying or entitled to occupy any part of the premises, be given access to those premises if it is reasonable to do so in connection with any matter arising out of the claim to the right to manage.[44]

Counter notice

9.55   Any person served with a notice of claim by an RTM company may give a counter notice within the time period allowed in the notice of claim. This will either consent to the RTM company acquiring the management on the date prescribed or allege that the RTM company is not entitled to acquire the management of the property.[45] Reasons must be given for making such an allegation.

9.56   There is a prescribed form available for counter notices as set out in the Right to Manage (Prescribed Particulars and Forms) (England)

---

43 See Right to Manage (Prescribed Particulars and Forms)(England) Regulations 2003 reg 4.

44 CLRA 2002 s83.

45 CLRA 2002 s82.

Regulations 2003.[46] This should be used as it contains statutory information that anyone serving a counter notice is required to provide to the RTM company.

9.57 If one or more counter notices are received which dispute the right of the RTM company to acquire the management of the property, an application may be made by the company to the LVT for a determination of this question. The onus is on the RTM company to take this step, as the right to manage cannot be exercised until this matter is determined or the person(s) who produced the counter notice give notice in writing of the withdrawal of their objections.

9.58 The RTM company must apply to the LVT for a determination that, on the relevant date, it was entitled to acquire the right to manage.[47] This application must be made within two months of the date of receipt of the last counter notice.

9.59 Reasons why a party may object to the exercise of the right to manage include:

• the building does not qualify;
• the RTM company does not comply with the legislative requirements;
• the members of the RTM company do not represent half the flats in the building.

9.60 The hearing before an LVT will simply be a question of whether or not the objections are true. If they are well founded and the RTM process is found to be flawed, the current application ceases to have effect and, if the defeated leaseholders wish to exercise the right to manage, must start the process again.

9.61 If an appeal is launched from the decision of an LVT, the RTM process is held in abeyance until the determination or abandonment of the appeal.[48]

Withdrawal of a claim notice

9.62 An RTM company may withdraw from the process at any time by service of a 'notice of withdrawal' on each person who is:[49]

a) a landlord under a lease;
b) a party to such a lease;

46 SI No 1988.
47 CLRA 2002 s82(3).
48 CLRA 2002 s82(7).
49 CLRA 2002 s86, 87.

c) a manager appointed under the LTA 1987;

d) a qualifying tenant.

9.63   An application is deemed to be withdrawn if, having received a counter notice, the RTM company does not apply for a determination of the issue by an LVT within two months, as set out above.[50]

9.64   If the RTM company makes the necessary application but then withdraws the application, the RTM process is deemed to have ceased. If the RTM company is wound up, struck off, enters into voluntary insolvency or has its assets compromised, the process is also deemed to have ceased.[51]

Costs of the RTM process

9.65   The RTM company is liable for the reasonable costs of the landlord, manager and other parties to the lease in respect of actions taken by them once a claim notice has been served.[52]

9.66   The costs of professional services (such as lawyers or accountants) are regarded as reasonable only to the extent that the person claiming them might reasonably have been expected to have incurred them and if he would be personally liable for those costs.[53] The RTM company is also liable for costs incurred by any such person in proceedings before the LVT if the LVT dismisses the application for a determination that it is entitled to acquire the right to manage.

9.67   In the event of a dispute about any costs claimed, the RTM company may apply to an LVT to have the matter determined.

9.68   If the RTM process is withdrawn, the general rule is that the RTM company is liable for the reasonable costs (as above) which have been incurred up to the date of withdrawal. Each person who is or has been a member of the RTM company is liable for those costs.[54]

---

50 CLRA 2002 s87(1).

51 CLRA 2002 s87(4).

52 CLRA 2002 s88.

53 CLRA 2002 s88(2).

54 CLRA 2002 s89.

Acquiring the right to manage

9.69 If there was no dispute as to the notice of claim, the RTM company acquires the right to manage on the date specified in the notice of claim.[55]

9.70 If there was a dispute which the LVT determined in favour of the RTM company, the acquisition date is three months after the determination becomes final.[56]

9.71 If the landlord could not be found and the RTM company made an application under CLRA 2002 s85 (see para 9.51), the acquisition date is as set out in the order made by the LVT.[57]

9.72 There are two further situations in which an RTM company may find itself involved with an LVT.

Duty to pay uncommitted service charges

9.73 Where a landlord has collected service charges in advance, but not yet spent them all, he is under an obligation to hand the sums over to the RTM company.[58] This does not require a notice from the RTM – the legislation places the duty firmly on the landlord, although it would be wise for the RTM company to remind him or her of this.

9.74 The sums must be paid on the acquisition date or as soon after as is reasonably practicable. The total sum will be calculated as follows:

• Monies paid by the leaseholders as service charges **plus** any interest or investment income generated by such money **less** the landlord's outgoings on the provision of services up to the acquisition date.

9.75 In the event that the landlord and RTM company cannot agree a figure, either party may apply to an LVT to determine the amount to be paid.

---

55 CLRA 2002 s90(2).
56 CLRA 2002 s90(4).
57 CLRA 2002 s90(6).
58 CLRA 2002 s94.

Approvals

9.76   Many leases provide for landlords to approve certain structural or other changes to the flats before tenants can act. Once the RTM is acquired, such consent can now validly be given by the RTM company.[46]

9.77   However, in any circumstance where consent is so needed, the RTM company must give at least 14 days' notice of its proposed decision to the landlord. This 14-day period rises to 30 days in the case of assignment, underletting, charging, parting with possession, the making of structural alterations or improvements or allocations of use.[47]

9.78   If, during the 14-/30-day notice period, the landlord objects, the RTM company may only grant its approval to the proposals if:[48]

a)   the person who objected later consents in writing; or
b)   the LVT determines that such consent should be given.

9.79   If the landlord does nothing during the 14-/30-day period, the RTM company may proceed as it wishes.

9.80   An application to the LVT for a determination of this question may be made by the RTM company, the tenant, any subtenant or the landlord.

9.81   The legislation is silent as to what criteria the LVT will use to make its decision although, given that this application can only arise if a landlord refuses to consent to the proposals, it seems likely that the test will be 'whether the landlord has acted reasonably in all the circumstances in refusing his consent'.

9.82   Presumably, in the case of structural alterations, proposals that would lower the value of the freehold will be rejected, as no reasonable landlord could be asked to consent to such activities. It also seems clear that tenants who have leases with only a short time left to run will find it more difficult to show that structural alterations are reasonable than those who have leases with a longer period to run.

59   CLRA 2002 s98(2).
60   CLRA 2002 s98(4).
61   CLRA 2002 s99(1).

CHAPTER 10

Forfeiture

Key points

- Leases often contain a provision that allows the landlord to bring the lease to an end if the tenant defaults on any obligation under the lease, including a covenant to pay service charges. This is known as 'forfeiture'.
- A court order is required before a lease can be deemed forfeit.
- Where the landlord is attempting to forfeit for failure to pay service charges, the service charge in dispute must have been determined by a court, LVT or arbitral tribunal.
- There are additional protections for tenants set out in Commonhold and Leasehold Reform Act (CLRA) 2002. These provisions have not yet been brought into force.

Introduction

10.1　Many leases have a provision which allows the landlord to bring the lease to an end if the tenant defaults on any of their covenants in the lease – including covenants to pay rent and service charges. This process is known as 'forfeiture'.

10.2　For many landlords forfeiture represents a convenient way to enforce a tenant's obligations but it is a power that is capable of creating a serious injustice. The tenant stands to lose their investment in their leasehold property, which may be out of all proportion to the damage suffered by the landlord.

10.3　This chapter will give a brief outline of the most relevant law and the provisions which exist to protect tenants of dwellings. It will then focus on the ways in which an LVT can be involved in deciding questions related to the forfeiture of a tenancy. Many of these protective provisions are only due to come into force with the 'accounting provisions' of the CLRA 2002, which is expected to be in Spring of 2005. The provisions which have yet to be brought into force will be clearly noted.

Outline of the law of forfeiture

10.4　Forfeiture is a very complicated topic which we will not attempt to cover in detail in this chapter; instead a very rough outline is given. A thorough (and very clear) account can be found in *Law of Real Property*.[1]

1　Megarry and Wade (Sweet & Maxwell, 6th edn, 1996) paras 14-118 onwards.

10.5   The common law makes a distinction between forfeiture for breach of covenant to pay rent and forfeiture for breach of any other covenant. The distinction arose because the damage to a landlord from a failure to pay rent can be calculated exactly and so courts were willing to order relief provided the tenant paid the arrears of rent and the landlord's costs.

Section 146 notices

10.6   This left tenants with no protection against forfeiture, where there was an alleged breach of a covenant other than one to pay rent. The Law of Property Act 1925 s146 gives statutory protection in those circumstances.

10.7   Where a landlord wishes to forfeit a lease because a tenant has breached a covenant, other than one to pay rent, the landlord will normally be required to serve a notice, called a section 146 notice, on the tenant. The notice must detail the breach of covenant that is complained of and give the tenant a reasonable time in which to remedy it. Only if the tenant fails to remedy the breach within that time, is the landlord permitted to forfeit the lease.

10.8   The landlord is not required to serve a section 146 notice if the breach of covenant by the tenant is not capable of being remedied, the thinking being that since the tenant cannot put the breach right, there is no point in asking them to do so. There is a great deal of case law as to what does and does not constitute an irremediable breach of covenant which we will not discuss here.

10.9   In the past a power to forfeit a lease was often expressed to be exercisable by 're-entry'. All a landlord needed to do was to re-enter the property peaceably and the lease would come to an end, though it could be brought back into existence if the tenant successfully applied to a court for relief against forfeiture.

10.10   In modern times forfeiture is almost always exercised by applying for an order for possession from a court. For tenants of a dwelling, a court order is compulsory before a lease is forfeit.[2] An attempt to evict a residential tenant unlawfully is both a tort[3] and a crime.[4]

---

2   Protection from Eviction Act 1977 s2.
3   Housing Act 1988 ss27–28.
4   Protection from Eviction Act 1977 s1.

Breach of covenant to pay rent

10.11   The rent that is due under long leases is often of a very small amount, perhaps tens of pounds every year. Where a landlord has been inactive a tenant might well inadvertently fail to pay the rent when it falls due. Under common law this gives the landlord the right to forfeit the lease and there is anecdotal evidence that some unscrupulous landlords have been deliberately waiting for tenants to pay late just so that they can exercise a power of forfeiture thus depriving their tenants of a valuable asset.

10.12   The accounting provisions of the CLRA 2002 will protect tenants in these circumstances in two ways: rent will not be due until it has been demanded by the landlord; and the landlord will not be permitted to exercise a right of forfeiture where only a small amount has been due for a short period of time.

10.13   Some leases 'reserve' service charge payments as rent, in which case a failure to pay service charges becomes a breach of covenant to pay rent for which a landlord may apply to a court to forfeit without first serving a section 146 notice. Where a court grants relief against forfeiture by ordering the tenant to pay all arrears of rent and the landlord's costs, the service charges owed will be treated as rent and would form part of the sum that the tenant had to pay.

10.14   Service charges are only treated as rent if they are expressly referred to as such in the lease.[5]

Notification that rent is due (not yet in force)

10.15   Once the accounting provisions of CLRA 2002 come into force a tenant will not be liable to pay any rent until the landlord has served a notice that rent is due on the tenant.[6] The notice must specify:

• the amount that is due;
• when it would have been due under the lease;
• a date for payment of the rent, which must be no earlier than when it would have been due under the lease and between 30 and 60 days (inclusive) after the service of the notice.

10.16   The tenant then becomes liable to pay the rent on the date specified in the notice. Here 'rent' does not include service or administration

---

5   *Khar v Delmounty Ltd* 75 P&CR 232 at 236.
6   CLRA 2002 s166.

charges[7] – where there will be more exacting requirements for notice and accounting (see chapter 3). It would appear that service charges are excluded even if they are reserved as rent.

10.17 The notice must be sent to the tenant at the dwelling, unless the tenant has notified the landlord of another address (which must be in England or Wales) to which notices that rent is due should be sent, in which case the landlord must send the notice to that other address.[8]

No forfeiture for failure to pay small amounts (not yet in force)

10.18 A landlord will also be prevented from bringing proceedings for forfeiture of the lease where a 'small amount' is owed for a 'small period' for either rent, service or administration charges.[9] The 'small amount' and 'small period' will be specified in regulations, though the 'small amount' can be no more than £500.[10] Draft regulations give a 'small amount' of £350, and a 'small period' of three years.[11]

10.19 The calculation of the amount owed excludes any 'default charge', that is an administration charge imposed for failure to pay rent, service or administration charges on time,[12] otherwise a landlord would be able to avoid the protection given to tenants by imposing default charges that would automatically take any arrears over the specified 'small amount'.

Breach of covenant to pay service charges

10.20 Even though a landlord may serve a section 146 notice on a tenant for failure to pay service charges, they may not go on to exercise their right of forfeiture until the amount of the service charge has been determined by a court, LVT or arbitral tribunal.[13]

10.21 The section 146 notice will itself be invalid unless it is accompanied by a notice that states that Housing Act 1996 s81 applies and the

---

7 CLRA 2002 s166(7).
8 CLRA 2002 s166(6).
9 CLRA 2002 s167.
10 CLRA 2002 s167(2).
11 Rights of Re-entry and Forfeiture (Prescribed Sum and Period) (England) Regulations 2004.
12 CLRA 2002 s167(3).
13 Housing Act 1996 s81.

effect of section 81(1) (that is, that the landlord will be prevented from exercising a right of forfeiture until the amount of service charge has been determined).[14]

10.22   The landlord is then prevented from exercising a right of forfeiture until 14 days after the decision of the court or tribunal. This right may be exercised at that time even if there is an appeal in progress against that decision.

New provisions (not yet in force)

10.23   When the accounting provisions of the CLRA 2002 come into force the protection for tenants will be improved in several ways:[15]

- Breach of covenant to pay administration charges is now covered by the same protection.[16]
- The landlord will be prevented from serving the section 146 notice until the amount of the service or administration charge has been determined. The section 146 notice may only be served after 14 days have elapsed from the final determination of the service or administration charge by a court or LVT, which will give the tenant further time to pay.[17]

10.24   A determination of a court or tribunal is not final until either all appeals have been exhausted or abandoned or the time to make an appeal (or subsequent appeal) has run out. This adds significantly to the amount of time by which a landlord can be delayed.[18]

Breach of other covenants (not yet in force)

10.25   When the relevant provisions of the CLRA 2002 come into force the jurisdiction of the LVT over forfeiture will be extended. A landlord of a long lease of a dwelling will not be permitted to serve a section 146 notice for a breach of covenant, other than one to pay service or administration charges,[19] until 14 days after a court or arbitral tribu-

---

14 Housing Act 1996 s82.
15 CLRA 2002 s170.
16 CLRA 2002 s170(2).
17 CLRA 2002 s170(3).
18 CLRA 2002 s170(4).
19 CLRA 2002 s169(7).

nal has determined that there has been a breach or the breach has been admitted by the tenant.[20]

10.26   A landlord may apply to an LVT for a determination that a breach of covenant has occurred.[21] As with breaches of covenant for failure to pay a charge, there is no final determination of a breach until all avenues of appeal have been exhausted or abandoned.

20   CLRA 2002 s168.
21   CLRA 2002 s168(4).

Leasehold Valuation Tribunal procedure

continued

Pre-action checklist

1 Check that your complaint is one that the LVT can deal with
Commentary
The most common complaints concern the payability of a service charge or administration charge; problems with insuring the property; the variation of a lease; and problems with a manager.

An LVT cannot order a landlord to pay money back to a tenant, nor can an LVT force a landlord to carry out repairs. Only a county court has this power.

2 Contact any other tenants who might be similarly affected
Commentary
Certain applications, such as those to appoint a manager, are more likely to be successful if tenants are in agreement about the problem and the remedy.

If there is more than one applicant, fees can be shared.

3 Write a letter to the landlord, manager, etc, setting out your concerns and asking how they plan to remedy them
Commentary
It may be that your problem can be resolved without the need for an LVT to get involved. In any event, attempts to be helpful and to resolve matters without coming before the LVT are factors which may be relevant to any decision an LVT makes about costs at the end of your case.

4 If the problem cannot be resolved and you need to apply to the LVT, check whether there is any specific procedure you must follow.
Commentary
This is the case with applications to appoint a manager, variation of a lease and most of the right to manage process. Failure to comply with the prescribed process may result in an LVT refusing to hear your case.

5 Complete the application form
Commentary
Not all applications have a prescribed application form. If there is no application form there is certain information that must be provided. See appendix C.

> The LVT process will now start. Consider what evidence you will need in order to prove your case and begin to collect it. There is no need to show the landlord your evidence at this stage. The LVT will set a date by when all evidence must be shown to the other side and given to the LVT.

Introduction

11.1   This chapter deals with how to make an application to the Leasehold Valuation Tribunal (LVT), and the progress of such an application through to a final determination.

11.2   Most LVT procedure is now governed by the Leasehold Valuation Tribunals (Procedure) (England) Regulations (LVT Regs) 2003[1] and the Leasehold Valuation Tribunals (Fees) (England) Regulations (Fees Regs) 2003.[2] No regulations have been made that encompass applications for the recognition of a tenants' association. As a matter of practice such applications will be treated by the LVT as being covered by the LVT and Fees Regs.

Starting a case

Ways in which a case comes before an LVT

11.3   The normal way for a case before an LVT to start is by one or more people making an application. In their application they will normally name one or more 'respondents' against whom they have brought the case.

11.4   An application does not need to be contentious. Sometimes all that is being done is asking an LVT to give official sanction to an agreement between landlord and tenants.

11.5   The other way that a case can come before an LVT is by transfer from the county court. The county court has the power to transfer cases to an LVT for a determination of issues which fall within its jurisdiction.[3] When this happens the claimant before the court

---

1   SI No 2099.
2   SI No 2098.
3   CLRA 2002 Sch 12 para 3.

becomes the applicant and the defendant becomes the respondent. The tribunal deals with these cases by asking the new applicant to fill in an application form. The case then proceeds much as it would have done if an application had been made directly, the only difference being in the treatment of fees (see para 11.34).

Before an application

11.6   There is no general requirement to go through any kind of pre-action protocol when dealing with an LVT, though some applications do have specific pre-action stages.

11.7   An LVT will take into account the behaviour of both the parties before an application and so it is to an applicant's advantage to try to come to an agreement with the other side and, unless matters are urgent, to write them a letter setting out formally the issues which will be raised with an LVT and asking if they can be resolved without recourse to the tribunal.

11.8   An applicant who springs a case on the respondent is likely to find an LVT unresponsive on the matter of costs, while a respondent who is unco-operative may not recover any costs even if they win.

Application forms

11.9   If at all possible, an application should be made on one of the LVT Service standard forms, which are available from the tribunal offices or the RPTS website.[4] Where there is no appropriate application form, a letter should be sent containing all the required information (see appendix C) to the LVT together with a statement that the applicant believes the information contained in the letter to be true.

Applicants

11.10   It is quite possible for several people to make the same application as joint applicants. This makes sense when each applicant wants an LVT to deal with essentially the same question. For example, where a number of tenants wish to challenge the same service charge demands. All of the tenants could apply on a single application form, attaching a list of all the applicants. From here on all that is said about 'an applicant' unless otherwise stated applies to a group of joint applicants.

4   www.rpts.gov.uk. See also appendix D.

11.11   It will often happen that the applicant wishes to raise a number of issues at the same time. For example, where a managing agent has behaved irresponsibly over a long period of time and an application is made for the appointment of a new manager. The applicant might also want to challenge service and administration charges that have been demanded. Application forms for each jurisdiction should be filled in and sent together. This has the advantage that only one application fee will be charged (see para 11.30). The most common application for a tenant to make is one under Landlord and Tenant Act (LTA) 1985 s20C for the tribunal to make an order preventing the landlord recovering the costs incurred in connection with LVT proceedings (see para 11.81). So common is it for a tenant to make an application under LTA 1985 s20C concurrently with one or more other applications that a tick box is supplied at the end of all application forms to allow a tenant applicant to do so. A tenant respondent would need to make a separate application for which there is as yet no application form.

Respondents

11.12   There is no requirement to name any particular individual(s) as respondent. It is advisable for applicants to name as respondents those who would be able to make a meaningful response to their application. For example, in a service charge case a tenant applicant might wish to name a managing agent as well as their landlord.

11.13   The tribunal will inform the respondents of the application and send them a copy of the application form.[5] The major exception to this is in variation of lease cases. Here the onus is on the applicant to make sure that all relevant parties have been informed of the application.[6] Failure to do so may allow those not informed to set aside any order made by the tribunal and sue for damages.[7]

Completing the application form

11.14   For all applications it is necessary to provide the address of the property and the name and address of the applicant as well as the name

5   LVT Regs 2003 reg 5(1).
6   LVT Regs 2003 reg 4.
7   LTA 1987 s39.

and address of respondent(s) and any other landlord or tenant not already given.[8] This should present no difficulties. If the name and address of the landlord is not known or some other information is not available, the tribunal has the power, providing it causes no prejudice, to waive any of the required information.[9]

11.15   The application forms are designed so that most of the form is common between jurisdictions.

11.16   The purpose of the application form is to help guide the tribunal with its case management and to decide whether a pre-trial review will be needed in order to properly organise the case. It is therefore important to set out clearly any matters which will affect the complexity of the case. It used to be common for applicants to send a large amount of paperwork with their application. This is now discouraged and all that should be sent is the minimum required by statute[10] (see appendix C) which will be clearly set out on the application form. If the tribunal requires any specific material to be sent in advance it will request such information by making a direction. If a case is likely to proceed without a pre-trial review and a party envisages that specific information should be sought then it should note this in a covering letter written to the tribunal and ask that a direction for the supply of the information be made.

11.17   If in any doubt as to the application procedure there is a national helpline for the Residential Property Tribunal Service on 0845 600 3178. They will not answer questions of a legal nature but do offer useful help with any administrative problems in dealing with the tribunal. Once an application has been made it is more appropriate to telephone or write to the clerk dealing with the case and ask for procedural advice.

11.18   The application form should be sent, together with any application fee (see para 11.25) to the relevant tribunal office. A list of tribunal offices, together with the regions they cover, can be found in appendix A. If an error is made and information is sent to the wrong office, it is likely that the LVT clerks will simply send it to the correct one. This will inevitably result in the application process being slowed by a few days.

---

8   LVT Regs 2003 reg 3(1).
9   LVT Regs 2003 reg 3(8).
10 LVT Regs 2003 Sch 2.

Fees

Free applications

11.19 The following applications do not require any fees to be paid:

- Determination of the payability of an estate management charge
- Variation of a lease on account of an estate management charge
- Variation of an estate management scheme
- No fault right to manage
- Application for costs not to be added to a service charge
- Recognition of a tenants' association

Payment of fees

11.20 The remainder of this chapter applies only to those applications which do not fall into this category. Where fees are payable they are the responsibility of the applicant and fall into two kinds: application fees and hearing fees. An application fee will always be payable; a hearing fee will only be charged in the event that there is a full hearing of the case. There is no hearing fee for pre-trial reviews or other preliminary hearings.[11] If the case is withdrawn or the tribunal rejects it at a preliminary hearing, there will be no hearing fee.

11.21 Fees are payable by the applicant and must be paid by cheque or postal order drawn in favour of the Office of the Deputy Prime Minister.[12] Cash will not be accepted. The application will not be considered complete unless it is accompanied by the application fee. Any application that is made without the relevant fee is likely to be rejected by the tribunal.

Waiver of fees

11.22 Those in receipt of the following benefits are entitled to have their fees waived:

- Income Support
- Housing Benefit
- Income Based Job Seeker's Allowance
- A working tax credit, and either:
  - the applicant or their partner receive a tax credit with a disability or severe disability element;

11 Fees Regs 2003 reg 1(3).
12 Fees Regs 2003 reg 6(3).

- – the applicant or their partner is also in receipt of a child tax credit;
- A guarantee credit under the State Pensions Credit Act 2002;
- A certificate issued under the Funding Code which has not been revoked or discharged and which is in respect of the proceedings before the tribunal the whole or part of which have been transferred from the county court for determination by a tribunal;
- A Working Tax Credit where the gross annual income used to calculate the Tax Credit is £14,213 or less.

11.23 An applicant's partner means either the applicant's spouse or a person of the opposite sex to the applicant with whom the applicant lives as husband and wife or a person of the same sex living with the applicant in a relationship which has the characteristics of the relationship between husband and wife.[13]

11.24 The tribunal supplies a special form to request a waiver of fees which should be completed and included with the application form. The waiver applies at the time any fee becomes payable and the tribunal should be kept informed of any changes in an applicant's circumstances.

Application fees

11.25 The amount payable by way of application fee varies. For applications in respect of charges, the amount of the fee depends on the value of charges that are the subject of the application; these fees are set out in Table A below. The wording of the regulations implies that the fee depends only on the amount of charge which is in question, so that if only part of a charge is disputed by an applicant they should make this clear on the application form so as to minimise the application fee.

11.26 Table A (overleaf) applies to applications to determine liability to pay a service charge; right to challenge the insurance premium; variation of a lease because of an administration charge and determination of liability to pay an administration charge.

11.27 The remaining chargeable applications depend on the number of dwellings that are the subject of the application; these fees are set out in Table B (overleaf) and apply to applications to dispense with consultation requirements, determination as to suitability of an insurer, appointment of managers and variation of leases.

13 Fees Regs 2003 reg 8(4)(b).

Table A

Charge which is the subject of the application	Application fee
not more than £500	£50
more than £500 but not more than £1,000	£70
more than £1,000 but not more than £5,000	£100
more than £5,000 but not more than £15,00	£200
more than £15,000	£350

Table B

Number of dwellings	Application fee
5 or fewer	£150
between 6 and 10	£250
more than 10	£350

Hearing fees

11.28   The hearing fee will usually be demanded in writing by the tribunal when a hearing date is set, which will usually be done by a direction issued after track allocation or at a pre-trial hearing review. Once demanded, the hearing fee is payable within 14 days of the demand.[14] The hearing fee is currently set at £150 for any application.[15]

11.29   The deadlines for payment are very strict. If a fee is more than one month late the tribunal will treat the application as withdrawn unless it is satisfied that there are reasonable grounds not to do so.[16]

Multiple applicants

11.30   If one person makes several applications at the same time, they need only pay the fee of the largest of them. This means it can be cost-effective to bring several applications together.

---

14   Fees Regs 6(2).
15   Fees Regs 5.
16   LVT Regs 7(2).

11.31   If there are several applicants, the fee is shared out between them. Joint tenants are counted as one person for the purposes of this apportionment. Where one or more applicants have had their fees waived only their share of the fee is waived. For example, suppose A and B are joint tenants of Flat 1, C is tenant of Flat 2 and D tenant of Flat 3 who has had his fee waived; A and B would each pay a sixth of the fee, C would pay one third and D would pay nothing.

11.32   Applicants who join later under LVT Regs 2003 reg 6 do not have to pay or contribute towards fees incurred before they join.[17]

11.33   Where several applications are heard together (perhaps because they have the same landlord or are part of the same large works project) the hearing fee is split equally between the applicants.[18]

Cases transferred from the county court

11.34   If the case is transferred to the LVT from the county court then the claimant in the county court becomes the applicant in the LVT and will be liable for application and hearing fees as they would if they had started the application in the LVT in the first place. However any court fees they have already paid to the county court will be credited to them and reduce their fees in the LVT accordingly.[19]

Track allocation

11.35   Cases will, in general, be dealt with in three ways or 'tracks' to borrow terminology from the Civil Procedure Rules. The three tracks are called: paper, fast and standard.

Paper track (case with no hearing)

11.36   The paper track is used for cases that are suitable for determination without a hearing. This avoids the expense of parties and their advisers having to attend a hearing and also has the advantage (for applicants) of there being no hearing fee to pay. The paper track may only be used with the written consent of all parties.[20] Parties who unreasonably refuse a paper track determination so as to put the other side

17 Fees Regs 7(6).
18 Fees Regs 2003 reg 7(4).
19 Fees Regs 2003 reg 4.
20 LVT Regs 2003 reg 13(1).

to the inconvenience of paying a hearing fee and attending a full hearing may find themselves in difficulty on the question of costs. There is no full hearing on the paper track; the case papers will be given to the tribunal at some point in a 'determination window' (usually one week long) when the case will be decided. The decision will then be communicated to the parties.

Fast track (case dealt with in 10 weeks)

11.37   The fast track aims to deal with all cases within 10 weeks. In consequence it will only be used for relatively simple cases where it is realistic to expect a fast turnaround. A case which is likely to require a full hearing of more than half a day is unlikely to be dealt with on the fast track. The tribunal's view of the appropriate track will take into account any previous experience of the parties' efficiency. Standard directions will be issued for all fast track cases (see para 11.44). In the event that these appear unsatisfactory parties should request a pre-trial review.

Standard track

11.38   Any application not suitable for the paper or fast tracks will be allocated to the standard track. This will be the most common track allocation. Directions can be tailored to suit the requirements of the individual case and in almost all circumstances a pre-trial review will be held. It is possible for an application to begin on the standard track and be reallocated after a pre-trial review.

11.39   Applicants are asked to suggest a track on the application form. The implication for applicants is that it is important to make clear on the application form any matters which might make a case unduly complicated or that might make it especially suitable for the fast track or a paper determination.

Pre-trial review

11.40   As explained above the tribunal will normally order a pre-trial review (PTR) for cases allocated to the standard track. A PTR may also be requested by the parties.[21] Unless specifically agreed otherwise, at least 14 days' notice of any such hearing must be given.[22] If a PTR is

21   LVT Regs 2003 reg 12.
22   LVT Regs 2003 reg 12(2).

listed it is important that the parties (or their representatives) attend. One of the key roles of a PTR is to set down dates for the service of evidence and the final hearing itself and it is important for each party to have considered any dates that they wish to avoid, perhaps due to long-standing commitments. Although tribunals are not required to list the final hearing at the convenience of the parties, in practice many attempt to do so.

11.41   A PTR is conducted by a 'Procedural Chair', who will not make rulings on questions of law or fact but exists solely to ensure that the dispute proceeds towards resolution with the least possible delay.

11.42   The purpose of the PTR is to:[23]

- give any directions that appear necessary or desirable in order to bring about the just, expeditious and economical disposal of proceedings;
- to secure and record all agreements and admissions that can reasonably be made in the proceedings;
- to record any refusal to make agreements or admissions.

11.43   Although the making and seeking of admissions is rare, parties should be aware that they are likely to be considered bound by any admissions they make at this stage and should consider their words carefully.

11.44   Directions mean the steps that must be taken before the final hearing date. Typically they should include:

- any amendments to the application;
- service of witness statements;
- provision for any expert evidence and the service of experts' reports;
- disclosure of documents;
- preparation of final hearing bundles.

11.45   Although the Chair is addressed as 'Sir' or 'Madam', the PTR is an informal setting and it is quite acceptable to ask for something to be explained or repeated, indeed, many Chairs make some considerable effort to check that all parties present have understood the terms of the directions being made.

11.46   The tribunal also has the power to postpone or adjourn a hearing or a PTR, either of its own initiative or at the request of any party. In considering whether to agree to a request for an adjournment or postponement, the tribunal must consider whether it can give reasonable

---

23 LVT Regs 2003 reg 12(3).

notice of any postponement or adjournment to the parties and, if this is possible, then it must be convinced that it would be reasonable to adjourn, having regard to:

- the grounds for the request;
- the time at which the request is made; and
- the convenience of the other parties.

11.47   If a request is made, all other parties are usually afforded the opportunity to comment. The tribunal is more likely to accept a request which is supported by all parties.

Interim matters

11.48   There are a number of other matters that may arise between the application and any final hearing or determination.

Joinder

11.49   A person may request to be joined as either an applicant or a respondent to an existing application.[24] This will often be because they feel that the application will touch on issues of direct concern to them. Such requests are normally considered on the face of the letter of request written by the requesting party. There does not appear to be a power to order oral submissions on whether to allow a joinder although there is no reason why the question could not be raised at a PTR. The existing parties will not usually be asked to comment on a request for joinder. A joined party becomes in almost every respect an applicant or respondent with all the rights and responsibilities that entails.

Dismissal without final hearing

11.50   The tribunal has the power to dismiss the whole or part of an application for being frivolous, vexatious or otherwise an abuse of process. A respondent may apply to the tribunal to dismiss an application, or the tribunal may make the decision of its own motion.[25]

11.51   Before dismissing an application the tribunal will give 21 days' notice for the applicant to request a hearing on the question of

24 LVT Regs 2003 reg 6.
25 LVT Regs 2003 reg 11.

whether the application be dismissed. The perceived objections to the application ought to be set out in some detail by the tribunal, so that the applicant is able to ascertain with sufficient certainty exactly what objections he must respond to. It is strongly recommended that applicants request a hearing in order to make submissions as to why the application be allowed to proceed in its current form. There is no fee for such a hearing.

11.52   If, after the oral hearing, the application is found to be frivolous, vexations or otherwise an abuse of process, or the applicant did not accept the invitation to attend an oral hearing, the application may be dismissed, in whole or part.[26]

11.53   Although not expressly mentioned in the regulations, tribunals have often treated themselves as having the power to allow amendments to applications. Frequently this was done at the PTR stage or, exceptionally, in the final hearing itself, as long as no prejudice was caused to any other parties. It may be that this practice will continue and, if a party feels that his application can be saved with an amendment, he would be wise to submit a text of the proposed amendment before the hearing date, with a copy going to the tribunal and any other interested parties.

Consolidation

11.54   The purpose of consolidation is to deal with a situation where a number of applications relate to substantially the same matters. It might be wasteful to deal with each application separately, especially if the same evidence were to be called in each case. It would also be possible for conflicting decisions to be made, which would be unsatisfactory.

11.55   If it appears to the tribunal that a number of applications have been made which relate to or include substantially the same matter(s), the tribunal may propose to determine one of the applications as being representative of all the common matters.[27]

11.56   If the tribunal comes to such a view, notice will be given to all the parties setting out the common matters; which application the tribunal intends to determine as the representative application; explaining that the findings in the representative application will be binding in all other cases and will invite comments, objections and observations on the tribunals proposal. There is a 21-day period for such objections.

11.57   Those who object, for any reason, will not be treated as being part

---

26   LVT Regs 2003 reg 11(4).
27   LVT Regs 2003 reg 8.

of the representative action and will continue their case as if the question of consolidation had not arisen, save that the representative action may be determined at the same time and possibly in the same hearing.

Withdrawal

11.58   There is no formal procedure for withdrawing an application, although as a matter of practice the LVT will accept an applicant's written request to do so.

Procedure at the final hearing

Inspections

11.59   It is common practice, often as an adjunct to the final hearing, for the LVT to inspect any property forming the subject of an application. The LVT may inspect any property that may have bearing on the application.[28] Advisers should consider whether to draw the LVT's attention to any neighbouring property.

11.60   A direction that inspection will take place will usually have been made at the pre-trial stage, if the LVT considered it would be useful. The purpose of such an inspection is to enable the LVT to see for itself items which are in dispute, such as, for example, the quality of workmanship where the sums charged are disputed.

11.61   If an inspection has been ordered it will usually take place on the morning of the final hearing. It is desirable for anybody planning to address the tribunal to be present at this visit because it is easier to make submissions at a final hearing on questions of workmanship or other issues of quality or necessity of work if all parties have seen the items in dispute.

11.62   No legal submission may be made at this point – all that parties are entitled to do is draw the tribunal's attention to matters which they consider relevant. The tribunal may ask parties questions during the site visit and it is quite proper to answer such questions, although as neutral a tone as possible should be adopted.

11.63   Parties are entitled to refuse access to their property to either the tribunal or any other party.[29] It would be unwise to do so as a tribunal

28   LVT Regs 2003 reg 17(1)(b).
29   LVT Regs 2003 reg 17(3).

is unlikely to be willing to inspect an area from which another party has been excluded.

Evidence

11.64   In most cases a direction for the disclosure of documents will have been made and it will usually be possible to obtain access to relevant documentation in the hands of other parties, though reasonable photocopying costs may be levied if there is a great deal of material. In cases where a party is obstructive or difficult the LVT has the authority to order the production of a document. Such an order should be requested in writing from the tribunal or at a pre-trial review.

11.65   Documentary evidence should be collected into a lever arch file (called a 'bundle'). It is sensible to arrange evidence in chronological order; to number each page and to put an index at the front. The tribunal will normally give a direction for the preparation of bundles and the supply of four copies to the tribunal (one each for the tribunal members and one for the clerk) and two to the other parties by a specified date.

11.66   Witnesses may give their evidence orally but it is now normal for their evidence to be prepared in writing in the form of a 'witness statement.' There are no rules for the preparation of witness statements but it is good practice for them to be written, signed and dated by the witness and consist of numbered paragraphs for ease of reference.

11.67   If parties have additional documentation on the day of the hearing they should give it to the clerk at the earliest opportunity, with a copy also being given to all parties present. If new documents are produced during the hearing, parties have the right to have an adjournment to give them time to consider the new evidence and for advisers to take instruction on it.[30] Such an adjournment is normally offered as a matter of course by the tribunal, though usually for a relatively brief period. Enough time should be given to allow a party sufficient opportunity to deal with the matters in the document.[31]

The final hearing

11.68   The proper approach to planning and presenting a case before the LVT is beyond the scope of this work and is well covered by general works on advocacy. This section highlights those features which are

30 LVT Regs 2003 reg 16(2).
31 LVT Regs 2003 reg 16(2).

peculiar to an LVT. The LVT is to a great extent free to organise its own procedure so that most of what is said here represents widespread practice. If in any doubt parties should ask the tribunal for guidance.

11.69   Assuming that inspection(s) have taken place in the morning, it is usual for the final hearing to start in the afternoon. Parties should make sure they arrive in good time. Final hearings usually take place in public before a three member panel.[32] The Chair, who will sit in the middle, will be legally qualified and be in charge of the conduct of proceedings. The other two members will usually not be lawyers although one of the tribunal must be experienced in the valuation of land. It is normal to address any remarks to the Chair unless one is answering a question addressed directly by one of the other members of the tribunal. There is no need to stand when making submissions. Unless otherwise stated, the tribunal members are addressed as 'Sir' or 'Madam' as appropriate.

11.70   All parties should have been given 21 days' notice of the final hearing date.[33] If one or more of the parties is not present at the final hearing, and the tribunal is satisfied that they had proper notice, then there is no objection to the final hearing continuing without their attendance.[34]

11.71   The tribunal may want to deal with one or more preliminary matters first, in particular where there is a question of jurisdiction. It is open to the tribunal to hear argument on that point before going on to the remainder of the final hearing.

11.72   When a party is presenting their case the normal structure is very similar to that used in the county court. A party may begin their case by making a short opening speech. This should be used to explain the structure of the case the applicant intends to present, especially if it is complicated. There is no need to say very much if the case is a simple one. The party then calls their witnesses in whatever order they choose. After giving evidence there will be an opportunity for other parties to cross-examine.

11.73   Tribunals are at least partly inquisitorial and they are likely to ask detailed questions of witnesses after cross-examination, though they will frequently ask questions at other times in order to clarify answers that have been given.

---

32 LVT Regs 2003 reg 14(6).
33 LVT Regs 2003 reg 14(3).
34 LVT Regs 2003 reg 14(8).

11.74   There is usually a seat set aside from which witnesses will give their evidence, although there is no witness box. It is normal for witnesses to sit when giving evidence and no oath is required. It is common for a tribunal to read a witness statement rather than requiring the witness to read it aloud. The applicant and the tribunal may ask supplementary questions to expand upon any points which might be unclear.

11.75   It is normal practice for the applicant to present their case first, followed by the respondent. For cases transferred from the county court the applicant will be the original claimant. It may be that it was the defendant (now the respondent) who first raised issues within the LVT's jurisdiction, it would seem to be more sensible in those circumstances for the respondent to start but it seems that not all tribunals are persuaded of this. If in doubt parties should ask the LVT what procedure they wish to adopt.

11.76   After all parties have presented their cases, each is usually allowed to make a final submission to the tribunal. The purpose is to summarise the evidence and explain what one's case is in the light of the evidence heard by the tribunal. The nature of the relief sought from the tribunal should also be made clear.

11.77   At the end of the hearing the question of costs should be raised. Both parties may wish to make submissions on the reimbursement of fees and what, if any, of their costs they should be awarded. Tenants should remember to make an application for protection against the landlord's costs, under LTA 1987 s20C (see para 11.81).

11.78   The decision of the tribunal may be given on the same day, but it is more common for the decision to be sent to the parties. The tribunal will usually indicate the approximate date by which the parties should expect the decision. If the decision contains a clerical error, omission, or other minor flaw, the tribunal should be contacted as they have the power to remedy such flaws after the decision has been handed down.[35]

Costs

11.79   Although, in the abstract, the tribunal has 'absolute discretion regarding costs',[36] a number of rules and practices have grown up over time. It is not automatic that the losing party pay the winner's costs. Instead,

---

35   LVT Regs 2003 reg 18(7).
36   *Langford Court v Doren* (2002) 5 JHLD 8.

the tribunal has a discretionary power to award up to £500 in costs if either the application is dismissed for being frivolous, vexatious or otherwise an abuse of process[37] or, in the tribunal's view, one of the parties has 'acted frivolously, vexatiously, abusively, disruptively or otherwise unreasonably in connection with the proceedings'.[38] Importantly this latter power can be applied regardless of who won and so, in theory, a successful party who behaved outrageously may end up having to pay some of the loser's costs.

11.80   The tribunal may also order a party to reimburse the whole or part of another party's application or hearing fees,[39] though such an order cannot be made against anyone who would have had their fees waived under LVT Regs 2003 reg 8. The tribunal will not consider exercising these powers unless asked.

11.81   This is not the end of the story as many leases give landlords the power to recover any costs incurred in connection with proceedings before an LVT from their tenants as an addition to their service charges. A tenant under such a lease could find themselves in the position of having won their case but having to pay all or some of their landlord's costs as an additional service charge. To avoid possible unfairness the LVT has a power under LTA 1987 s20C to prevent the landlord exercising any such power.

11.82   To rely on LTA 1987 s20C, the tenant must seek such protection from the LVT. This should normally be done by ticking the appropriate box at the end of the application form. In circumstances where this has not or cannot be done (for example, where the tenant is the respondent) a separate application (which is free) should be made to the LVT. We recommend a brief letter to this effect which should be copied to the other parties. The letter must specify by name those whom the tenant wishes to be protected under section 20C. There is nothing to stop such an application being made after a hearing has been concluded and the decision given, although a late application may be regarded with less sympathy.

11.83   It is normal for the LVT to hear argument as to whether or not to grant a request made under LTA 1987 s20C at the end of the final hearing. The tribunal will make such an order as it considers just and equitable in all the circumstances[40]. Criteria which have been thought to be important in the past include:

37 LVT Regs 2003 reg 11.
38 CLRA 2002 Sch 12 para 10.
39 Fees Regs 2003 reg 9.
40 LTA 1985 s20C(3).

- Whether any party suggested any form of alternative dispute resolution and, if so suggested, the reaction of the other parties.
- Offers of settlement.[41]
- The reasonableness of any consultation period or process.
- Whether an itemised breakdown of legal costs has been provided.
- The fact that the tribunal is designed to be 'user friendly', with no requirement for legal representation.
- The presumption that the majority of Local Authorities use their own in-house legal team.
- The importance of ensuring that prospective applicants are not deterred by a fear of costs orders against them.
- The degree to which parties complied with the directions, if any, made at the pre-final hearing review.
- Whether any party unreasonably refused to agree to allocate the dispute to the paper track.

11.84　In the event that costs are awarded in favour of a tenant, protection under LTA 1987 s20C should be granted as a matter of course.[42]

11.85　On all questions of costs, it should be remembered that the 'philosophy of the LVT (is) as an accessible, low cost vehicle for the hearing and resolution of disputes.'[43] A tribunal will not be sympathetic to those who amass considerable costs bills without very good reason.

Appeals

11.86　An appeal from a decision of an LVT may be made to the Lands Tribunal.[44] Such an appeal may only be made with the permission of the LVT or the Lands Tribunal.[45] Where permission is sought from an LVT the application for permission must be made within 21 days of the date on which the document recording the reasons for the decision to be appealed was made.[46]

---

41 *Loder Dyer v Cadogan* [2001] EGLR 149.
42 *Holding and Management Ltd v Property Holding and Investment Trust plc* [1989] 1 WLR 1313, 1324 per Nicholls LJ. Affirmed in *Iperion Investments v Broadwalk House Resident Ltd* (1995) 46 EG 188.
43 *Southerland v Hounslow* LVTP/SC/032/126/02; LVTP/SCC/032/068/02, Chair Jane Dowell. This decision contains an excellent overview of the relevant factors.
44 CLRA 2002 s175.
45 CLRA 2002 s175(2).
46 LVT Regs 2003 reg 20.

11.87   The procedural rules for appeals to the Lands Tribunal are set out in the Lands Tribunal Rules 1996[47] as amended and supplemented by the Practice Directions of 5 April 2001. It is advisable to read these documents. Lands Tribunal procedure is not within the scope of this book.

---

47 SI No 1022.

Worked examples

Appointment of a manager

Background

12.1   Anderson House is a block of six flats, all of which are owned by Ms Broome. She has given long leases of all six flats to six different tenants. The leases are all substantially similar. Anderson House is managed by Ms Broome personally.

12.2   Tenant 1 is dissatisfied with Ms Broome's management. She rarely visits Anderson House, fails to return Tenant 1's phone calls and has failed to consult Tenant 1 before having the common areas of Anderson House repainted. Tenant 1's lease expressly required him to be consulted about any internal improvements or repairs.

Pre-application process

12.3   Tenant 1 speaks to Tenants 2, 3, 4 and 5, all of whom agree with Tenant 1's complaints about Ms Broome. Tenant 6 does not wish to get involved.

12.4   Tenants 1, 2, 3, 4 and 5 write a joint letter to Ms Broome. setting out their complaints. They ask her to contact them within 28 days to discuss the problem. Ms Broome never replies. (See Fig 1 below).

12.5   Tenants 1, 2, 3, 4 and 5 decide that Ms Broome is not someone they want to be responsible for managing the property. They visit their local Citizens Advice Bureau and discover that the LVT may have the power to order that a new manager be appointed.

12.6   They check that their property is one over which the LVT has power. Their property is one with more than two flats and does not fall within any of the exemptions set out in the Landlord and Tenant Act 1987.

12.7   Confident that the LVT could grant them the remedy that they want, they write to Tenant 6, saying that they want to have a new manager appointed. Tenant 6 replies that he has no firm views and does not want to get involved.

12.8   They check to see whether there is anything they must do before applying to the LVT. They discover that there is a pre-application process set out in the Landlord and Tenant Act 1987.

12.9   Firstly they must send a 'preliminary notice' to the landlord and anyone else who has management duties under the lease. They check their leases and discover that only the landlord, Ms Broome, has management duties, although she has a power to appoint a managing agent if she wants.

12.10 They therefore have to send a preliminary notice to the landlord. Luckily, they have her address and send the preliminary notice by recorded delivery. They ask Ms Broome to contact them within 28 days in order to discuss their concerns. (See Fig 2 below).

12.11 Ms Broome replies that she has better things to do than answer endless letters from the tenants and that the common areas clearly needed repainting. She cannot understand why the tenants are complaining.

12.12 The tenants decide that nothing else can be achieved without an order of the LVT.

The LVT application

12.13 There is no prescribed application form, so the tenants produce a document setting out their case. They complain that Ms Broome is in breach of her management obligations under the lease. She is given the duty to manage the property by the lease and, although she is entitled to appoint a managing agent if she wishes, that duty remains hers. By failing to consult the tenants before having the common areas repainted, she was in breach of an obligation under the lease.

12.14 They also allege that, by failing to answer their letters and return their phone calls, she has been in breach of the code of practice of the Royal Institute of Chartered Surveyors (RICS).

12.15 The LVT receives the application, together with the relevant fee. They inform Ms Broome of the application and list a pre-trial review (PTR). The tenants and Ms Broome are each given at least 14 days' notice of the PTR.

The pre-trial review

12.16 At the PTR only tenants 1, 2, 3 and 4 can attend. Tenant 5 has work commitments. Ms Broome also attends. Tenant 1 is appointed to speak on behalf of the applicants.

12.17 The PTR gives the tenants and Ms Broome dates by which they must serve any evidence, including any witness statements. The tenants are ordered to produce a short-list of three possible managers that they agree on. The case is listed for a final hearing.

12.18 The tenants have to pay a hearing fee of £150.

Evidence

12.19   The tenants send in the following evidence:

- witness statements from tenants 1, 2, 3, 4 and 5 setting out their specific complaints against Ms Broome, together with copies of the letters that they say she did not answer;
- copies of their leases, showing Ms Broome's duty to consult them before painting the common areas;
- a list of three possible managers. They suggest tenant 1 as their first choice manager, and two professional management companies as second and third choices;
- a letter from tenant 6 saying that, while he is not a part to this application, he has no objection to tenant 1 or a professional manager being appointed;
- letters from the two professional management companies stating that they would be willing to take over the management of the property and setting out their likely fees.

12.20   Ms Broome sends in a witness statement explaining that she has been very busy with other commitments and apologises for not answering the letters. She promises to be a better manager in the future.

The hearing

12.21   Tenant 1 speaks on behalf of the other tenants. They all confirm that their witness statements are true and that they want tenant 1 to be the manager for the property.

12.22   Ms Broome again apologises for the problems. She complains that having tenant 1 as a manager would not be fair to her as she fears that there is now bad blood between her and the tenants. She says that she wants to be a better manager of her property and promises that these problems would not occur again.

12.23   When asked by the LVT, she says that, if she could not stay as manager, she would prefer to have a professional manager appointed, rather than tenant 1.

12.24   The LVT adjourned to consider it's decision.

The decision

12.25   Shortly after the hearing, the tenants and Ms Broome are sent a copy of the LVT's decision.

12.26   The LVT referred itself to Landlord and Tenant Act 1987 s24. It found that, by not consulting the tenants before having the common area repainted, Ms Broome had been in breach of a management obligation under the lease. It also accepted that by failing to answer letters and return phone calls, Ms Broome was in breach of the RICS code of property management.

12.27   However, it noted that Ms Broome was apparently sincere in her desire to be a better property manager. It noted that tenant 1 had no experience in property management and that neither tenant 6 nor Ms Broome had any objection to a professional manager being appointed. In these circumstances, the LVT felt that it would not be 'just and convenient' to appoint tenant 1, but rather appointed one of the companies suggested by the tenants.

12.28   The company was appointed for two years and was appointed to carry out all the management duties of Ms Broome, as set out in the lease. As the tenants had been substantially successful, Ms Broome was ordered to refund their application fees.

Fig 1 – Letter before action

Tenants 1, 2, 3, 4, 5
Anderson House
London
AB12 3CD

Ms Broome
Landlord Road
London
EF45 6GH   20 June 2004

Dear Ms Broome,

We are contacting you concerning the following problems arising out of your management of Anderson House.

(1) We have each individually attempted to contact you in the recent past to discuss various matters, but have been unable to reach you. It appears that you are unable or unwilling to return our telephone calls or acknowledge our letters

(2) Under clause 2(a) of our leases, you are required to consult us before carrying out any internal improvements or repairs. The common areas of our property have recently been repainted without you having consulted us.

We are anxious to discuss matters with you to ensure that these problems do not occur again in the future. Please contact us within 28 days of the date of this letter in order that we might arrange a mutually convenient time to meet and discuss the situation.

Yours sincerely

Tenants of Anderson House

Fig 2 – Preliminary notice

Tenants 1, 2, 3, 4, 5
Anderson House
London
AB12 3CD

Ms Broome
Landlord Road
London
EF45 6GH

20 Aug 2004

Dear Ms Broome,

We last contacted you on 20 June 2004 and received no reply. For your convenience, a copy of that letter is enclosed.

This is a preliminary notice under section 22 of the Landlord and Tenant Act 1987. Please address all correspondence to 'Tenants 1, 2, 3, 4, 5, Anderson House, London, AB12 3CD.

We intend to make an application for an order that a manager be appointed for Anderson House.

You are currently exercising the management functions. It is our view you have failed to comply with clause 2(a) of our leases. By this clause you are required to consult us before carrying out any internal improvements or repairs. The common areas of our property have recently been repainted without you having consulted us. A copy of the lease is attached to this letter.

In addition, you have failed to return our numerous phone calls and letters relating to our concerns about your management of Anderson House.

We would hope that these matters can be resolved without the need for litigation. To assist in achieving this, we ask that you contact us within 28 days of the date of this letter.

If there is an mortgage secured on Anderson House, you must provide the mortgagee with a copy of this notice.

Yours sincerely

Tenants of Anderson House

Service charge dispute

Background

12.29   Illingworth Housing Association has granted a long lease of 1 Black-acre Road to Ms Gill. Service charges are collected each year without any difficulties and are generally in the region of £2,500–3,000 a year.

12.30   In 2004, Ms Gill receives a service charge demand for £10,000. Three items listed on the breakdown of costs provided by Illingworth Housing Association concern her. She has been charged £2,000 for new plants in her garden, £3,000 for cleaning services throughout the year and £1,500 for a new fence to be erected.

12.31   She feels that these charges are excessive and complains to Illingworth Housing Association. In reply, the housing association point out that, under the lease, all service charge demands are payable within 28 days. Unless the sums are paid, they will bring a case in the county court to recover the sums owed and may even attempt to forfeit her lease. (See Fig 3 below).

12.32   Ms Gill takes legal advice and discovers that, in her case, the LVT has a power to determine whether or not these service charges are payable by her to Illingworth Housing Association. She writes to the housing association stating that she is willing to discuss payment proposals with them, but, if the dispute cannot be resolved amicably, she will issue proceedings in the LVT.

12.33   Illingworth Housing Association reply that, in their view, the work billed for has all been done and was all subject to competitive tender. She should therefore pay the sums demanded.

12.34   Ms Gill applies to the LVT for a determination of the payability of her 2004 service charge bill. She is aware that her lease allows Illingworth Housing Association to recover its legal costs from her, and so asks the LVT for an order that this not be allowed to happen, as well as a determination of her service charge dispute.

12.35   Ms Gill is in receipt of Job Seekers' Allowance and so has her application fee waived.

12.36   The LVT contacts Illingworth Housing Association to inform them of the application and lists a PTR.

12.37   The PTR gives Ms Gill and Illingworth Housing Association dates by which they must serve any evidence, including any witness statements. Ms Gill, as she was in receipt of Job Seekers allowance, was also exempt from any hearing fee.

Evidence

12.38 Ms Gill submitted a copy of her lease, along with a witness statement setting out her case.

12.39   Illingworth Housing Association submitted evidence of their tendering process, showing that the companies that provided the cleaning services and the new fence had been chosen after a competitive and open tendering process.

The hearing

12.40 Ms Gill has submitted her witness statement as requested. Her case is:

a) £2,000 for new plants is not payable because nowhere in her lease is Illingworth Housing Association given responsibility for tending the gardens. This has always been a tenant's own duty.

b) £3,000 for cleaning services is excessively expensive. She could get cleaners who would do the job for £1,000.

c) The fence only cost £1,500 because it had to be replaced. In fact it had been deteriorating for years and if it had been repaired when it first began to show signs of wear, it would have been cheaper.

12.41 Illingworth HA have submitted their witness statement. Their case is:

a) The lease gives them a power to 'improve the general amenity of the property and recover any charges associated in so doing from the tenant.'

b) £3,000 was a fair rate for commercial cleaners.

c) The Housing Association had a policy of replacing all fences every seven years. There was no evidence that the fence should have been repaired earlier. £1,500 was a fair price for a new fence.

12.42 The LVT asked for an inspection of Ms Gill's property on the morning of the hearing. This request was accepted by Ms Gill. The LVT was particularly interested in comparing Ms Gill's fence to those of her neighbours who had not had their fences replaced.

12.43   The hearing resumed in the afternoon. The LVT decided to deal with each of the three issues in turn.

12.44   Ms Gill explained that tenants had always had responsibility for their own gardens. Illingworth Housing Association accepted that this had been the past practice, but pointed to the clause in the lease.

12.45   When asked questions by the LVT and he housing association, Ms Gill explained that she had no concerns about the quality of the cleaning but had been told by a friend who did some part-time cleaning, that £1,000 would be a fair figure. Illingworth Housing Association relied on their tendering process, but, when questioned by Ms Gill, accepted that there had been some lower tenders.

12.46   On the fence, Ms Gill repeated her allegation that, had the fence been replaced earlier, it would have been cheaper. She accepted that she had no evidence to support this. Illingworth Housing Assocation again relied on their tendering process and denied that the fence could have been replaced for less if it had been done earlier.

12.47   The LVT indicated that it would give its decision in writing later. However, it wanted to hear submissions on whether or not to allow the housing association to recover its costs from Ms Gill.

12.48   Illingworth Housing Association submitted that they had been put to expense attending and that they should be able to recover this from Ms Gill.

12.49   Ms Gill pointed to her early letters, where she had offered to negotiate the situation without the need for any LVT hearing. Had this been taken up, she said, no costs would have needed to be incurred.

Decision

12.50   The LVT sent a written decision to Ms Gill and Illingworth Housing Association shortly afterwards. When dealing with the service charge application, the LVT reminded itself that it had to determine whether or not the amounts claimed were payable.

a)   On the £2,000 for new plants, the LVT found that the lease did not allow Illingworth Housing Association to recover these costs. The clause relied on by the housing association did not expressly refer to the gardens. Clauses of this nature had to be read restrictively. As such, none of the £2,000 was payable.

b)   On the £3,000 for cleaning, the LVT noted that Ms Gill had accepted that there was no concern over the quality of the work. Illingworth Housing Association was entitled to use commercial cleaners. It did not have to rely on what independent people might charge for cleaning. In any event, Ms Gill had not provided any documentary evidence to support her figure of £1,000. However, using its own local knowledge, the LVT did feel that £3,000 was slightly expensive and substituted a figure of £2,500.

c)   On the £1,500 for the new fence, while the LVT had some sympathy for the argument that it might have been cheaper had the work been done earlier, there was no evidence at all to support this. £1,500 seemed to be a fair figure based on the evidence available to the LVT.

Accordingly, the LVT found a total of £4,000 to be payable.

12.51   The LVT decided to grant Ms Gill protection against having to pay Illingworth Housing Association's costs. It was impressed by her early offer to discuss and negotiate the matter and the fact that the housing association had declined to even explore this opportunity should be held against them.

Fig 3 – Letter before action

Ms S Gill
1 Blackacre Road
Manchester
IJ78 9JL

Illingworth Housing Association
College Street
Manchester
MN10 9PQ   20 June 2004

Dear Sir or Madam,

Re: Service charge demand – your ref: 00897436

I am a long leaseholder of 1 Blackacre Road. I have recently received a demand for service charges from you in respect of my property. The total bill is for £10,000. I have identified three items on the bill that I am unclear about. For your ease of reference, these are:

(1) £2,000 for new plants in my garden;
(2) £3,000 for cleaning services;
(3) £1,500 for a new fence.

I believe the sums demanded to be excessive. I would appreciate your comments as to how each sum has been calculated. In particular, I would ask for your comments on the following:

(1) Tenants have, during the whole of my time as a tenant, been responsible for their own gardens. Why have Illingworth Housing Association now decided (a) to do work in the gardens and (b) to charge for this work?
(2) £3,000 is excessively expensive. I have been told that £1,000 is a fair price for cleaning charges and I do not see why I should pay more than this.
(3) Had the fence been repaired when problems first became apparent, it would not have cost £1,500 as this is the cost of a new fence.

I look forward to hearing from you at your earliest convenience and, in any event, within 28 days of the date of this letter.

Yours sincerely

Ms S Gill

APPENDICES

Useful addresses

TRIBUNAL OFFICES

London Rent Assessment Panel

Residential Property Tribunal Service
10 Alfred Place
London WC1E 7LR

Tel: 020 7446 7700
Fax: 020 7637 1250
Email: london.rap@odpm.gsi.gov.uk
DX: 134205 Tottenham Court Road 2

This office covers all the London boroughs.

Northern Rent Assessment Panel

Residential Property Tribunal Service
20th Floor
Sunley Tower
Piccadilly Plaza
MANCHESTER
M1 4BE

Tel: 0845 100 2614
Fax: 0161 237 3656
Email: northern.rap@odpm.gsi.gov.uk

This office covers the following Metropolitan districts: Bolton, Bury, Manchester, Oldham, Rochdale, Salford, Stockport, Tameside, Trafford, Wigan, Knowsley, Liverpool, St Helens, Sefton, Wirral, Barnsley, Doncaster, Rotherham, Sheffield, Gateshead, Newcastle upon Tyne, North Tyneside, South Tyneside, Sunderland, Bradford, Calderdale, Kirklees, Leeds and Wakefield.

It also covers the following unitary authorities: Hartlepool, Middlesborough, Redcar and Cleveland, Darlington, Halton, Blackburn with Darwen, Blackpool, Kingston upon Hull, East Riding of Yorkshire, North-east Lincolnshire, North Lincolnshire, Stockton-on-Tees, Warrington and York.

It also covers the following counties: Cheshire, Cumbria, Durham, Lancashire, Lincolnshire.

Midland Rent Assessment Panel

Residential Property Tribunal Service
2nd Floor
East Wing
Ladywood House
45–46 Stephenson Street
BIRMINGHAM B2 4DH

Tel: 0845 100 2615
Fax: 0121 643 7605
Email: midland.rap@odpm.gsi.gov.uk

This office covers the following metropolitan districts: Birmingham, Coventry, Dudley, Sandwell, Solihull, Walsall, Wolverhampton.

It also covers the following unitary authorities: Derby, Leicester, Rutland, Nottingham, Herefordshire, Telford and Wrekin and Stoke on Trent. It also covers the following counties: Derbyshire, Leicestershire, Nottinghamshire, Shropshire, Staffordshire, Warwickshire and Worcestershire.

Eastern Rent Assessment Panel

Residential Property Tribunal Service
Great Eastern House
Tenison Road
CAMBRIDGE CB1 2TR

Tel: 0845 100 2616
Fax: 01223 505116
Email: eastern.rap@odpm.gsi.gov.uk

This office covers the following unitary authorities: Bracknell Forest, West Berkshire, Reading, Slough, Windsor and Maidenhead, Wokingham, Luton, Peterborough, Milton Keynes, Southend on Sea, Thurrock.

It also covers the following counties: Bedfordshire, Buckinghamshire, Cambridgeshire, Essex, Hertfordshire, Norfolk, Northamptonshire, Oxfordshire and Suffolk.

Southern Rent Assessment Panel

Residential Property Tribunal Service
1st Floor
1 Market Avenue
CHICHESTER
PO19 1JU

Tel: 0845 100 2617
Fax: 01243 779389
Email: southern.rap@odpm.gsi.gov.uk

This office covers the following unitary authorities: Bath and North-east Somerset, Bristol, North Somerset, South Gloucestershire, Bournemouth, Plymouth, Torbay, Poole, Swindon, Medway, Brighton and Hove, Portsmouth, Southampton and the Isle of Wight.

It also covers the following counties: Cornwall and the Isles of Scilly, Devon, Dorset, East Sussex, Gloucestershire, Hampshire, Kent, Somerset, Surrey, West Sussex and Wiltshire.

OTHER USEFUL CONTACT DETAILS

Association of Retirement Housing Managers
3rd Floor
89 Albert Embankment
London SE1 7TP

Tel: 020 7820 1839
Fax: 020 7820 1839
E-mail: enquiries@arhm.org

Royal Institute of Chartered Surveyors
RICS Contact Centre
Surveyor Court
Westwood Way
Coventry CV4 8JE

Tel: 0870 333 1600
E-mail: contactrics@rics.org

Companies House
Crown Way
Maindy
Cardiff CF14 3UZ

Tel: 0870 33 33 636
E-mail: enquiries@companies-house.gov.uk

Tribunal Representation Service
College of Law
14 Store Street
London WC1E 7DE

Tel: 020 7291 1230
Fax: 020 7291 1348
E-mail: ssadvice.centre@lawcol.co.uk

LEASE – the Leasehold Advisory Service
70–74 City Road
London EC1Y 2BJ

Tel: 0845 345 1993
Fax: 020 7253 2043
E mail: info@lease-advice.org

The telephone lines are open Monday to Friday from 9:30am until 1pm and from 2pm until 3:30pm.

USEFUL WEBSITES

LEASE   www.lease-advice.org
RPTS   www.rpts.gov.uk
Companies House   www.companieshouse.gov.uk
Association of Retirement Housing Managers   www.arhm.org
Royal Institute of Chartered Surveyors   www.rics.org
Lands Tribunal   www.landstribunal.gov.uk

Standing

WHO MAY APPLY TO AN LVT

A question that is often raised by applicants and their advisers is whether a particular individual is entitled to apply to the LVT. The answer will depend on the particular jurisdiction being exercised by the LVT. In some cases there are legislative provisions which restrict who may apply. Even where there is no restriction, an LVT has the power to strike out a frivolous application under Leasehold Valuation Tribunals (Procedure) (England) Regulations 2003 reg 11.[1]

The table covers all the jurisdictions of the LVT covered in this book, and indicates who may apply under that jurisdiction.

LVT jurisdictions – who may apply

Provision	Description	Applicant
Service charges		
LTA 1985 s27A	Determination of liability to pay service charge.	Anyone.
LTA 1985 s20ZA	Dispensation from consultation requirements.	Anyone.
LTA 1985 s21A	Determination that landlord has a reasonable excuse for a failure giving rise to the tenants right to withhold service charges.	Landlord[2] (includes any person who has a right to enforce payment of service charges).[3]
LTA 1985 s20C	Order that costs in connection with LVT proceedings should not be regarded as relevant costs.	Tenant.[4]

1   SI No 2099.
2   If an RTM company has acquired the right to manage, the RTM company has the right instead of the landlord, CLRA 2002 Sch 11 para 4(2).
3   LTA 1985 s30.
4   Includes a landlord under a lease of the whole or any part of the premises if an RTM company has acquired the right to manage, CLRA 2002 Sch 11 para 4(3).

Provision	Description	Applicant
Administration charges		
CLRA 2002 Sch 11 para 3	Variation of administration charge provision in a lease.	Any party to the lease.[5]
CLRA 2002 Sch 11 para 5	Liability to pay an administration charge.	Anyone.
Estate charges		
CLRA 2002 s159(3)	Variation of estate charge provisions in an estate management scheme.	Any person on whom an obligation to pay an estate charge is imposed by the scheme.
CLRA 2002 s159(6)	Determination of payability of an estate charge.	Anyone.
Variation of leases		
LTA 1987 s35	Application to vary a long lease.	A party to the lease.[6]
LTA 1987 s36	Application to vary another lease in response to a LTA 1987 s35 application to vary a long lease.	A party to the LTA 1987 s35 lease.
LTA 1987 s37	Application to vary two or more leases.	Landlord or any tenant of the leases.
LTA 1987 s39(3)(b)	Application for the cancellation or modification of an order varying a lease.	A person on whom a notice was required to be served under LTA 1987 s35(5).
Variation of insurance provisions		
LTA 1987 s40(1)	Variation of the insurance provisions of a dwelling.	Party to the lease.
Challenge to the landlord's choice of insurer		
LTA 1985 Sch para 8	Challenge to the landlord's choice of insurer.	Landlord[7] or tenant.[8]

---

5 Includes an RTM company, if it has acquired the right to manage, CLRA 2002 Sch 11 para 16.
6 Includes an RTM company, if it has acquired the right to manage, CLRA 2002 Sch 11 para 10.
7 If an RTM company has acquired the right to manage in respect of the premises, the RTM company instead of the landord, CLRA 2002 Sch 11 para 5(2).
8 Includes a landlord under a lease of the whole or any part of the premises who is under an obligation to make payments under CLRA 2002 s103 (landlord's contribution to service charges), CLRA 2002 Sch 11 para 5(3).

Provision	Description	Applicant
Appointment of managers		
LTA 1987 s24(1)	Order appointing a manager.	Tenant.[9]
LTA 1987 s24(9)	Variation or discharge of order appointing a manager.	Any person interested.
LTA 1987 s22(3)	Order dispensing with requirement to serve a preliminary notice before applying for appointment of a manager.	Anyone.
Right to manage		
CLRA 2002 s84(3)	Determination that an RTM company was entitled to acquire the right to manage in response to a counter-notice.	The RTM company.
CLRA 2002 s85(2)	Order that an RTM company is to acquire the right to manage where the landlord is missing.	The RTM company.
CLRA 2002 s88(4)	Determination of any question arising in relation to the costs payable by an RTM company.	Anyone.
CLRA 2002 s94(3)	Determination of amount of payment of accrued uncommitted service charges.	(1) Any party, other than a tenant, of a lease of the whole or part of the premises. (2) A manager appointed under LTA 1987 Part 2. (3) The RTM company.
CLRA 2002 s99(1)	Determination of whether an approval is to be given under the terms of the lease.	The RTM company, landlord, tenant or subtenant (where the approval is to be given by a tenant).
CLRA 2002 Sch 6 para 5(3)	Determination that right to manage may be exercised earlier than four years.	The RTM company.
Forfeiture		
CLRA 2002 s168(4)	Determination that a breach of covenant or other condition in the lease has occurred.	Landlord.

9   Includes a landlord under a lease of the whole or any part of the premises, where an RTM company has acquired the right to manage, CLRA 2002 Sch 11 para 8(3).

Information to be provided in all applications

All applications must include the following information:

- the name and address of the applicant;
- the name and address of the respondent;
- the name and address of any landlord or tenant of the property to which the application relates.
- the address of the premises to which the application relates;
- a statement that the applicant believes the facts stated in the application to be true.

In addition, each application has further specified requirements.

Service charge, administration charge and estate charge applications

- A copy of the lease/estate management scheme must always be included.
- If the application is to determine the payability of service charges, the name and address of any recognised tenant's association must be included.
- If the application is to vary an administration charge, a draft of the proposed variation must be included.

Estate management schemes

- A copy of the existing estate management scheme or proposed estate management scheme must always be included.
- Any proposed variation to an estate management scheme must include a description of the proposed variation, including identification of the area by a map or plan.

Appointment of manager

- Where a preliminary notice was served, a copy of that notice.
- Where the application is to vary an existing management order, a copy of the earlier order must be provided.

Variation of leases

- The name and address of all persons who were served with notice of proposed variation.
- A draft of the proposed variation must be provided.

Right to manage

- Any application relating to the right to manage must include the name and address for service of the RTM company, the name and address of the freeholder, any intermediate landlord and manager and a copy of the memorandum and articles of association of the RTM company.
- Where the application is by the RTM company to determine whether, following the receipt of a counter notice, it was entitled to acquire the right to manage, a copy of the claim notice and any counter notices must be provided.
- Where the RTM company is unable to trace a landlord and applies to the LVT to determine whether it can acquire the right to manage, a statement must be served showing that the notice inviting participation and the notice of claim were fulfilled and a copy of the notice served on all qualifying tenants must also be provided. The reasons why the landlord cannot be identified and traced should also be set out.
- Where the application relates to uncommitted service charges, an estimate of the value of the accrued but uncommitted service charges must be provided.
- Where the RTM company wishes to grant an approval for works or the like without going through the prescribed process and applies to the LVT for dispensation, a copy of the lease must be provided.
- Where the RTM company applies for a determination that, although the right to manage has lapsed, the RTM company should still be permitted to exercise the right to manage, the RTM company must set out the date and circumstances in which the right to manage ceased.

Residential Property Tribunal Service application forms

**Residential
Property**
TRIBUNAL SERVICE

**Application Form
S27A Landlord and Tenant Act 1985**
Application for a determination of liability to pay service charges

This is the correct form to use if you want the Leasehold Valuation Tribunal to determine the liability to pay any service charge. This includes the question of whether or not the service charge is reasonable.

Please do not send any documents with this application form except a copy of the lease. If and when further evidence is needed you will be asked to send it in separately. If you have any questions about how to fill in this form or the procedures the Tribunal will use, please call us on 0845 600 3178. **Please send this completed application form together with the application fee and a copy of the lease to the appropriate panel (see page 6 for panel addresses).**

1. DETAILS OF APPLICANT(S) (if there are multiple Applicants please continue on a separate sheet)

Name _____

Address (including postcode) _____

_____

_____

Address for correspondence *(if different)* _____

_____

Telephone: *Day:* _____ *Evening:* _____ *Mobile:* _____

Email address: _____

Capacity (e.g. landlord/tenant/managing agent) _____

Representative details _____

_____

_____

Where details of a representative have been given, all correspondence and communications will be with them until the tribunal is notified that they are no longer acting.

2. ADDRESS (including postcode) OF PROPERTY (if not already given)

_____

_____

_____

3. BRIEF DESCRIPTION OF PROPERTY *(e.g., 2-bedroom flat in Victorian block)*

_____

_____

_____

1

4. DETAILS OF RESPONDENT(S) (if there are multiple Respondents please continue on a separate sheet)

Name _____

Address (including postcode) _____

_____

_____

_____

Address for correspondence *(if different)* _____

_____

_____

_____

Telephone: *Day:* _____ *Evening:* _____ *Mobile:* _____

Email address *(if known)*: _____

Capacity *(e.g. landlord/tenant/managing agent)* _____

5. DETAILS OF LANDLORD (if not already given)

Name _____

Address (including postcode) _____

_____

_____

Telephone: *Day:* _____ *Evening:* _____ *Mobile:* _____

Email address *(if known)*: _____

6. DETAILS OF ANY RECOGNISED TENANTS' ASSOCIATION (if known)

Name of Secretary _____

Address (including postcode) _____

_____

_____

Telephone: *Day:* _____ *Evening:* _____ *Mobile:* _____

Email address *(if known)*: _____

7. SERVICE CHARGES TO BE CONSIDERED BY THE TRIBUNAL

a. **Service charges for past years**

Please list years for which a determination is sought

1. _____ 2. _____

3. _____ 4. _____

5. _____ 6. _____

For each service charge year, fill in one of the sheets of paper entitled **Service Charges in Question.**

b. **Service charges for current or future years**

Please list years for which a determination is sought

1. _____ 2. _____

3. _____ 4. _____

5. _____ 6. _____

For each service charge year, fill in one of the sheets of paper entitled **Service Charges in Question.**

8. OTHER APPLICATIONS

Do you know of any other cases involving either: (a) the same or similar issues about the service charge as in this application; or (b) the same landlord or tenant or property as in this application ? If so please give details.

_____

_____

_____

9. LIMITATION OF COSTS

If you are a tenant, do you wish to make a s20C application *(see Guidance Notes)*   YES ☐   NO ☐

If so, why? _____

_____

_____

Guidance Notes
Some leases allow a landlord to recover costs incurred in connection with the proceedings before the LVT as part of the service charge.
Section 20C of the Landlord and Tenant Act 1985 gives the tribunal power, on application by a tenant, to make an order preventing a landlord from taking this step. If you are a tenant you should indicate here whether you want the tribunal to consider making such an order.

10. CAN WE DEAL WITH YOUR APPLICATION WITHOUT A HEARING?

If the Tribunal thinks it is appropriate, and all the parties agree, it is possible for your application to be dealt with entirely on the basis of written representations and documents and without the need for parties to attend and make oral representations. This means you would not be liable for a hearing fee of £150 but it would also mean that you would not be able to explain your case in person. Please let us know if you would be happy for your application to be dealt with in this way.

I would be happy for the case to be dealt with
on paper if the Tribunal thinks it is appropriate   YES ☐   NO ☐

NB: Even if you have asked for a determination on paper the Tribunal may decide that a hearing is necessary. Please go on to answer questions 11 to 13 on the assumption that a hearing will be heard.

11. TRACK PREFERENCES

We need to decide whether to deal with the case on the Fast Track or the Standard Track.
(see Guidance Notes for an explanation of what a track is). Please let us know which track you think appropriate for this case.

Fast Track ☐   Standard Track ☐

Is there any special reason for urgency in this case?   YES ☐   NO ☐

If there is, please explain how urgent it is and why: _____
_____
_____

The Tribunal will normally deal with a case in one of three ways: on paper, on the "fast track", and on the "standard track." The fast track is designed for cases that need a hearing but are very simple and will not generate a great deal of paperwork or argument. A fast track case will usually be heard within 10 weeks of your application. You should indicate here if you think the case is very simple and can easily be dealt with. The standard track is designed for more complicated cases where there may be numerous issues to be decided or where, for example, a lot of documentation is involved. A standard track case may involve the parties being invited to a Pre-Trial Review which is a meeting at which the steps that need to be taken to bring the case to a final hearing can be discussed.

12. AVAILABILITY

If there are dates or days we must avoid during the next three months (either for your convenience or the convenience of any expert you may wish to call) please list them here.

Dates on which you will NOT be available _____
_____
_____

13. VENUE REQUIREMENTS

Please provide details of any special requirements you or anyone who will be coming with you may have (e.g., the use of a wheelchair and/or the presence of a translator) _____
_____
_____

In London cases are usually heard in Alfred Place, which is fully wheelchair accessible. Elsewhere hearings are held in local venues which are no all so accessible and the Clerks will find it useful to know if you or anyone you want to come to the hearing with you has any special requirements of this kind.

4

14. CHECK LIST

Please check that you have completed this form fully. The tribunal will not process your application until this has been done and it has both a copy of the lease and the application fee:

A copy of the lease(s) is/are enclosed ☐

A crossed cheque or postal order for the application fee (if applicable) is enclosed ☐

Amount of fee enclosed _____ Please put your name and address on the back of any cheque you send.

DO NOT send cash under any circumstances. Cash payment will not be accepted and any application accompanied by cash will be returned to the applicant.

Please ONLY send this application form, a copy of the lease and the application fee and nothing else.

Guidance notes:
The amount of the application fee will depend on the total amount of service charge that is in dispute. To find out how much you will need to pay you should consult the following table:

Amount of Service Charge in dispute	Application Fee
Not more than £500	£50
More than £500 but less than £1,000	£70
More than £1,000 but less than £5,000	£100
More than £5,000 but less than £15,000	£200
More than £15,000	£350

Fees should be paid by a crossed cheque made payable to or a postal order drawn in favour of the Office of the Deputy Prime Minister.

Waiver and Fees
*You will **not** be liable to pay a fee if you or your partner is in receipt of:*
* *Income Support*
* *Housing Benefit*
* *Income Based Job Seeker's Allowance*
* *A working tax credit, and either:*
  * *you or your partner receive a tax credit with a disability or severe disability element; or*
  * *you or your partner is also in receipt of a child tax credit*
* *a guarantee credit under the State Pensions Credit Act 2002*
* *certificate issued under the Funding Code which has not been revoked or discharged and which is in respect of the proceedings before the tribunal the whole or part of which have been transferred from the county court for determination by a tribunal*
* *A Working Tax Credit where the Gross Annual Income used to calculate the Tax Credit is £14,213 or less*

If you wish to claim a waiver of fees you must complete another form available from the Panel office. The waiver form will not be copied to other parties in the proceedings.

If you are making several applications at the same time, even if you are using different application forms or the applications relate to different parts of the Tribunal's jurisdiction, you do not have to pay a separate fee for each application. The overall fee will be the biggest of the fees payable for each application on its own.

If you are in any doubt about the amount of fee or have any other questions about how to fill in this form please telephone the RPTS help line on 0845 600 3178.

15. STATEMENT OF TRUTH

I believe that the facts stated in this application are true. _____

Signed: _____ Dated: _____

5

PANEL ADDRESSES

Northern Rent Assessment Panel
20th Floor, Sunley Tower, Piccadilly Plaza, Manchester M1 4BE

Telephone: 0845 1002614
Facsimile: 0161 2367 3656

Midland Rent Assessment Panel
2nd Floor, East Wing, Ladywood House
45-46 Stephenson Street
Birmingham B2 4DH

Telephone: 0845 1002615
Facsimile: 0121 643 7605

Eastern Rent Assessment Panel
Great Eastern House, Tenison Road, Cambridge CB1 2TR

Telephone: 0845 1002616
Facsimile: 01223 505116

London Rent Assessment Panel
2nd Floor, 10 Alfred Place, London WC1E 7LR

Telephone 020 7446 7700
Facsimile 020 7637 1250

Southern Rent Assessment Panel
1st Floor, 1 Market Avenue, Chichester PO19 1JU

Telephone: 0845 1002617
Facsimile: 01243 779389

6

SERVICE CHARGES IN QUESTION

PLEASE USE THE SPACE BELOW TO PROVIDE INFORMATION REGARDING EACH OF THE YEARS MENTIONED IN PART 7 OF THE MAIN APPLICATION FORM.

You will be given an opportunity later to give further details of your case and to supply the Tribunal with any documents that support it. At this stage you should give a clear outline of your case so that the Tribunal understands what your application is about.

The year in question _____

A list of the items of service charge that are in issue (or relevant) and their value _____

_____

_____

_____

_____

_____

_____

Description of the question(s) you wish the tribunal to decide _____

_____

_____

_____

_____

_____

_____

_____

_____

Any further comments you may wish to make _____

_____

_____

_____

_____

_____

_____

_____

_____

Residential Property
TRIBUNAL SERVICE

Ref no. (for office use only)

Application Form
Schedule 11 to the Commonhold and Leasehold Reform Act 2002
Application for the determination of the liability to pay or for
the variation of an administration charge

This is the correct form to use if you want to ask the Leasehold Valuation Tribunal to determine liability to pay an administration charge or to vary an administration charge under paras. 5 or 3 of Schedule 11 to the Commonhold and Leasehold Reform Act 2002.

Please do not send any documents with this application form except a copy of the lease and any other documents required by paragraph 6 of this form. If and when further evidence is needed you will be asked to send it in separately. If you have any questions about how to fill in this form or the procedures the Tribunal will use, please call us on 0845 600 3178. **Please do not send any documents with this application except a copy of the lease and any other documents required by paragraph 6 of this form.**

1. DETAILS OF APPLICANT(S) (if there are multiple Applicants please continue on a separate sheet)

Name _____

Address (including postcode) _____

_____

_____

Address for correspondence *(if different)* _____

_____

Telephone: *Day:* _____ *Evening:* _____ *Mobile:* _____

Email address: _____ Fax: _____

Capacity (e.g. landlord/tenant/managing agent) _____

Representative details _____

_____

_____

Where details of a representative have been given, all correspondence and communications will be with them until the tribunal is notified that they are no longer acting.

2. ADDRESS (including postcode) OF PROPERTY (if not already given)

_____

_____

_____

3. BRIEF DESCRIPTION OF PROPERTY *(e.g., 2-bedroom flat in Victorian block)*

_____

_____

_____

1

4. DETAILS OF RESPONDENT(S) (if there are multiple Respondents please continue on a separate sheet)

Name _____

Address (including postcode) _____

_____

_____

Address for correspondence *(if different)* _____

_____

_____

Telephone: *Day:* _____ *Evening:* _____ *Mobile:* _____

Email address *(if known)*: _____

Capacity *(e.g. landlord/tenant/managing agent)* _____

5. DETAILS OF LANDLORD (if not already given)

Name _____

Address (including postcode) _____

_____

Telephone: *Day:* _____ *Evening:* _____ *Mobile:* _____

Email address *(if known)*: _____

2

6. ADMINISTRATION CHARGES TO BE CONSIDERED BY THE TRIBUNAL

This form may be used for applications for the determination of the liability to pay an administration charge or for the variation of an administration charge.

Please provide the following information on the attached sheet entitled "Administration Charge Details" or provide the details in a separate document.

(a)   the date of the lease;

(b)   the clauses under which the administration charge is demanded

(c)   the grounds of the claim;

Complete a separate sheet for each administration charge challenged.

Please enclose the following documents with the application form:

(a)   Copies of the relevant lease(s);

(b)   The demand (s) for the administration charge;

(c)   If you wish to ask the LVT to vary the administration charge clause in the lease, a draft of the variation.

Guidance Note
An administration charge is an amount payable by a tenant of residential property:
(a) in connection with the grant of an approval under the lease or an application for such an approval;
(b) in connection with the provision of information or documents by, or on behalf of, the landlord or some other party to the lease;
(c) in respect of a failure to make a payment by the due date to the landlord or another party to the lease;
(d) in connection with a breach (or alleged breach) of a covenant or condition in the lease.
Administration charges can be variable or fixed. A variable charge is one that is neither specified in the lease nor is calculated in accordance with a formula specified in the lease. The LVT has power only to vary fixed administration charges

7. OTHER APPLICATIONS

Do you know of any other cases involving either: (a) the same or similar issues about an administration charge as in this application; or (b) the same landlord or tenant or property as in this application? If so please give details.

_____

_____

_____

_____

8. LIMITATION OF COSTS

If you are a tenant, do you wish to make a s20C application *(see Guidance Notes)*   YES ☐   NO ☐

If so, why? _____

_____

_____

Guidance Notes
Some leases allow a landlord to recover costs incurred in connection with the proceedings before the LVT as part of the service charge. Section 20C of the Landlord and Tenant Act 1985 gives the tribunal power, on application by a tenant, to make an order preventing a landlord from taking this step. If you are a tenant you should indicate here whether you want the tribunal to consider making such an order.

9. CAN WE DEAL WITH YOUR APPLICATION WITHOUT A HEARING?

If the Tribunal thinks it is appropriate, and all the parties agree, it is possible for your application to be dealt with entirely on the basis of written representations and documents and without the need for parties to attend and make oral representations. This means you would not be liable for a hearing fee of £150 but it would also mean that you would not be able to explain your case in person. Please let us know if you would be happy for your application to be dealt with in this way.

I would be happy for the case to be dealt with
on paper if the Tribunal thinks it is appropriate   YES ☐   NO ☐

NB: *Even if you have asked for a determination on paper the Tribunal may decide that a hearing is necessary. Please go on to answer questions 11 to 13 on the assumption that a hearing will be heard.*

10. TRACK PREFERENCES

We need to decide whether to deal with the case on the Fast Track or the Standard Track.

(see Guidance Notes for an explanation of what a track is). Please let us know which track you think appropriate for this case.

Fast Track ☐   Standard Track ☐

Is there any special reason for urgency in this case? YES ☐   NO ☐

If there is, please explain how urgent it is and why: _____

_____

_____

The Tribunal will normally deal with a case in one of three ways: on paper, on the "fast track", and on the "standard track." The fast track is designed for cases that need a hearing but are very simple and will not generate a great deal of paperwork or argument. A fast track case will usually be heard within 10 weeks of your application. You should indicate here if you think the case is very simple and can easily be dealt with. The standard track is designed for more complicated cases where there may be numerous issues to be decided or where, for example, a lot of documentation is involved. A standard track case may involve the parties being invited to a Pre-Trial Review which is a meeting at which the steps that need to be taken to bring the case to a final hearing can be discussed.

11. AVAILABILITY

If there are dates or days we must avoid during the next three months (either for your convenience or the convenience of any expert you may wish to call) please list them here.

Dates on which you will NOT be available _____

_____

_____

12. VENUE REQUIREMENTS

Please provide details of any special requirements you or anyone who will be coming with you may have (e.g., the use of a wheelchair and/or the presence of a translator) _____

_____

In London cases are usually heard in Alfred Place, which is fully wheelchair accessible. Elsewhere hearings are held in local venues which are not all so accessible and the Clerks will find it useful to know if you or anyone you want to come to the hearing with you has any special requirements of this kind.

13. CHECK LIST

Please check that you have completed this form fully. The tribunal will not process your application until this has been done. Please ensure that the following are enclosed with your application:

A copy of the lease(s) is/are enclosed ☐

A copy of the demand(s) for the administration charge(s) is/are enclosed ☐

A draft of the variation sought (if applicable) is enclosed ☐

A crossed cheque or postal order for the application fee (if applicable) is enclosed ☐

Amount of fee enclosed _____ Please put your name and address on the back of any cheque you send.

DO NOT send cash under any circumstances. Cash payment will not be accepted and any application accompanied by cash will be returned to the applicant.

Please ONLY send this application form, a copy of the lease and the application fee and nothing else.

Guidance notes:
The amount of the application fee will depend on the total amount of administration charge that is in dispute. To find out how much you will need to pay you should consult the following table:

Amount of Administration Charge in dispute	Application Fee
Not more than £500	£50
More than £500 but not more than £1,000	£70
More than £1,000 but not more than £5,000	£100
More than £5,000 but not more than £15,000	£200
More than £15,000	£350

Fees should be paid by a crossed cheque made payable to or a postal order drawn in favour of the Office of the Deputy Prime Minister.

Waiver and Fees
You will not be liable to pay a fee if you or your partner is in receipt of:
* *Income Support*
* *Housing Benefit*
* *Income Based Job Seeker's Allowance*
* *A working tax credit, and either:*
  * *you or your partner receive a tax credit with a disability or severe disability element; or*
  * *you or your partner is also in receipt of a child tax credit*
* *a guarantee credit under the State Pensions Credit Act 2002*
* *a certificate issued under the Funding Code which has not been revoked or discharged and which is in respect of the proceedings before the tribunal the whole or part of which have been transferred from the county court for determination by a tribunal*
* *A Working Tax Credit where the Gross Annual Income used to calculate the Tax Credit is £14,213 or less*

If you wish to claim a waiver of fees you must complete another form available from the Panel office. The waiver form will not be copied to other parties in the proceedings.

If you are making several applications at the same time, even if you are using different application forms or the applications relate to different parts of the Tribunal's jurisdiction, you do not have to pay a separate fee for each application. The overall fee will be the biggest of the fees payable for each application on its own.

If you are in any doubt about the amount of fee or have any other questions about how to fill in this form please telephone the RPTS help line on 0845 600 3178.

14. STATEMENT OF TRUTH

I believe that the facts stated in this application are true.

Signed: _____ Dated: _____

5

PANEL ADDRESSES

Northern Rent Assessment Panel
20th Floor, Sunley Tower, Piccadilly Plaza, Manchester M1 4BE

Telephone: 0845 1002614
Facsimile: 0161 237 3656

Midland Rent Assessment Panel
2nd Floor, East Wing, Ladywood House
45-46 Stephenson Street
Birmingham B2 4DH

Telephone: 0845 1002615
Facsimile: 0121 643 7605

Eastern Rent Assessment Panel
Great Eastern House, Tenison Road, Cambridge CB1 2TR

Telephone: 0845 1002616
Facsimile: 01223 505116

London Rent Assessment Panel
2nd Floor, 10 Alfred Place, London WC1E 7LR

Telephone 020 7446 7700
Facsimile 020 7637 1250

Southern Rent Assessment Panel
1st Floor, 1 Market Avenue, Chichester PO19 1JU

Telephone: 0845 1002617
Facsimile: 01243 779389

ADMINISTRATION CHARGE DETAILS

PLEASE USE THE SPACE BELOW TO PROVIDE INFORMATION MENTIONED IN PART 6 OF THE MAIN APPLICATION FORM.

You will be given an opportunity later to give further details of your case and to supply the Tribunal with any documents that support it. At this stage you should give a clear outline of your case so that the Tribunal understands what your application is about. Please continue on a separate sheet if necessary.

Please tick one of the following:

This is an application for the determination of the liability to pay an administration charge ☐

This is an application for the variation of an administration charge ☐

Now complete the rest of this form

The date and term of the lease(s) _____

The relevant paragraphs of the lease(s) _____

The grounds for the application _____

A draft of the variation sought (if applicable) _____

**Residential
Property**
TRIBUNAL SERVICE

**Application Form
Section 20ZA of the Landlord and Tenant Act 1985**
Application for the dispensation of all or any of the consultation
requirements contained in section 20 of the Landlord and Tenant Act 1985

This is the correct form to use if you want the Leasehold Valuation Tribunal to determine the liability to pay any service charge. This includes the question of whether or not the service charge is reasonable.

1. DETAILS OF APPLICANT(S) (if there are multiple Applicants please continue on a separate sheet)

Name _____

Address (including postcode) _____

_____

_____

_____

Address for correspondence *(if different)* _____

_____

_____

Telephone: *Day:* _____ *Evening:* _____ *Mobile:* _____

Email address: _____ *Fax:* _____

Capacity (e.g. landlord/tenant/managing agent) _____

Representative details _____

_____

_____

Where details of a representative have been given, all correspondence and communications will be with them until the tribunal is notified that they are no longer acting.

2. ADDRESS (including postcode) OF PROPERTY (if not already given)

_____

_____

_____

3. BRIEF DESCRIPTION OF PROPERTY *(e.g., 2-bedroom flat in Victorian block)*

_____

_____

_____

4. DETAILS OF RESPONDENT(S) (if there are multiple Respondents please continue on a separate sheet)

Name _____

Address (including postcode) _____

_____

_____

Address for correspondence *(if different)* _____

_____

_____

Telephone: *Day:* _____ *Evening:* _____ *Mobile:* _____

Email address *(if known)*: _____

Capacity *(e.g. landlord/tenant/managing agent)* _____

Guidance Note

Guidance note: if this is an application by a landlord, then usually all tenants liable to pay a service charge for the costs in question should be joined as respondents. If tenants are not joined in this way then the landlord should provide the tribunal with a list of the names and addresses of service charge payers. If this is not possible or is impractical then a written explanation must be provided with this application.

5. DETAILS OF LANDLORD (if not already given)

Name _____

Address (including postcode) _____

_____

Telephone: *Day:* _____ *Evening:* _____ *Mobile:* _____

Email address *(if known)*: _____

6. DETAILS OF ANY RECOGNISED TENANTS' ASSOCIATION (if known)

Name of Secretary _____

Address (including postcode) _____

_____

Telephone: *Day:* _____ *Evening:* _____ *Mobile:* _____

Email address *(if known)*: _____

2

7. DISPENSATION SOUGHT

Applicants may seek a dispensation of all or any of the consultation requirements in respect of either qualifying works or long term agreements.

Does the application concern qualifying works ?   YES ☐   NO ☐

If yes, have the works started/been carried out ?   YES ☐   NO ☐

Does the application concern a qualifying long-term agreement?   YES ☐   NO ☐

If yes has the agreement already been entered into?   YES ☐   NO ☐

For each set of qualifying works and/or qualifying long agreement please complete one of the sheets of paper entitled **Grounds for seeking dispensation.**

8. OTHER APPLICATIONS

Do you know of any other cases involving either: (a) related or similar issues about the service charge as in this application; or (b) the same landlord or tenant or property as in this application? If so please give details.

_____

_____

_____

9. LIMITATION OF COSTS

If you are a tenant, do you wish to make a s20C application *(see Guidance Notes)*   YES ☐   NO ☐

If so, why? _____

_____

Guidance Notes
Some leases allow a landlord to recover costs incurred in connection with the proceedings before the LVT as part of the service charge. Section 20C of the Landlord and Tenant Act 1985 gives the tribunal power, on application by a tenant, to make an order preventing a landlord from taking this step. If you are a tenant you should indicate here whether you want the tribunal to consider making such an order.

3

10. CAN WE DEAL WITH YOUR APPLICATION WITHOUT A HEARING?

If the Tribunal thinks it is appropriate, and all the parties agree, it is possible for your application to be dealt with entirely on the basis of written representations and documents and without the need for parties to attend and make oral representations. This means you would not be liable for a hearing fee of £150 but it would also mean that you would not be able to explain your case in person. Please let us know if you would be happy for your application to be dealt with in this way.

I would be happy for the case to be dealt with
on paper if the Tribunal thinks it is appropriate   YES ☐   NO ☐

NB: *Even if you have asked for a determination on paper the Tribunal may decide that a hearing is necessary. Please go on to answer questions 11 to 13 on the assumption that a hearing will be heard.*

11. TRACK PREFERENCES

We need to decide whether to deal with the case on the Fast Track or the Standard Track.
(see Guidance Notes for an explanation of what a track is). Please let us know which track you think appropriate for this case.

Fast Track ☐   Standard Track ☐

Is there any special reason for urgency in this case?   YES ☐   NO ☐

If there is, please explain how urgent it is and why: _____
_____
_____

The Tribunal will normally deal with a case in one of three ways: on paper, on the "fast track", and on the "standard track." The fast track is designed for cases that need a hearing but are very simple and will not generate a great deal of paperwork or argument. A fast track case will usually be heard within 10 weeks of your application. You should indicate here if you think the case is very simple and can easily be dealt with. The standard track is designed for more complicated cases where there may be numerous issues to be decided or where, for example, a lot of documentation is involved. A standard track case may involve the parties being invited to a Pre-Trial Review which is a meeting at which the steps that need to be taken to bring the case to a final hearing can be discussed.

12. AVAILABILITY

If there are dates or days we must avoid during the next three months (either for your convenience or the convenience of any expert you may wish to call) please list them here.

Dates on which you will NOT be available _____
_____
_____

13. VENUE REQUIREMENTS

Please provide details of any special requirements you or anyone who will be coming with you may have (e.g., the use of a wheelchair and/or the presence of a translator) _____
_____
_____

In London cases are usually heard in Alfred Place, which is fully wheelchair accessible. Elsewhere hearings are held in local venues which are not all so accessible and the Clerks will find it useful to know if you or anyone you want to come to the hearing with you has any special requirements of this kind.

4

14. CHECK LIST

Please check that you have completed this form fully. The tribunal will not process your application until this has been done. Please ensure that the following are enclosed with your application:

A copy of the lease(s) is/are enclosed ☐

Service charge payers have been named as respondents or a list of names and addresses has been provided ☐

A crossed cheque or postal order for the application fee (if applicable) is enclosed ☐

Amount of fee enclosed _____ Please put your name and address on the back of any cheque you send.

DO NOT send cash under any circumstances. Cash payment will not be accepted and any application accompanied by cash will be returned to the applicant.

Please ONLY send this application form, a copy of the lease and the application fee and nothing else.

Guidance notes:
The amount of the application fee will depend on the number of dwellings to which the application relates. To find out how much you will need to pay you should consult the following table:

Number of dwellings to which application relates	Application Fee
5 or fewer dwellings	£150
Between 6 and 10 dwellings	£250
More than 10 dwellings	£350

Fees should be paid by a crossed cheque made payable to or a postal order drawn in favour of the Office of the Deputy Prime Minister.

Waiver and Fees
*You will **not** be liable to pay a fee if you or your partner is in receipt of:*
* *Income Support*
* *Housing Benefit*
* *Income Based Job Seeker's Allowance*
* *A working tax credit, and either:*
  * *you or your partner receive a tax credit with a disability or severe disability element; or*
  * *you or your partner is also in receipt of a child tax credit*
* *a guarantee credit under the State Pensions Credit Act 2002*
* *a certificate issued under the Funding Code which has not been revoked or discharged and which is in respect of the proceedings before the tribunal the whole or part of which have been transferred from the county court for determination by a tribunal*
* *A Working Tax Credit where the Gross Annual Income used to calculate the Tax Credit is £14,213 or less*

If you wish to claim a waiver of fees you must complete another form available from the Panel office. The waiver form will not be copied to other parties in the proceedings.

If you are making several applications at the same time, even if you are using different application forms or the applications relate to different parts of the Tribunal's jurisdiction, you do not have to pay a separate fee for each application. The overall fee will be the biggest of the fees payable for each application on its own.

If you are in any doubt about the amount of fee or have any other questions about how to fill in this form please telephone the RPTS help line on 0845 600 3178.

15. STATEMENT OF TRUTH

I believe that the facts stated in this application are true.

Signed: _____ Dated: _____

PANEL ADDRESSES

Northern Rent Assessment Panel
20th Floor, Sunley Tower, Piccadilly Plaza, Manchester M1 4BE

Telephone: 0845 1002614
Facsimile: 0161 2367 3656

Midland Rent Assessment Panel
2nd Floor, East Wing, Ladywood House
45-46 Stephenson Street
Birmingham B2 4DH

Telephone: 0845 1002615
Facsimile: 0121 643 7605

Eastern Rent Assessment Panel
Great Eastern House, Tenison Road, Cambridge CB1 2TR

Telephone: 0845 1002616
Facsimile: 01223 505116

London Rent Assessment Panel
2nd Floor, 10 Alfred Place, London WC1E 7LR

Telephone 020 7446 7700
Facsimile 020 7637 1250

Southern Rent Assessment Panel
1st Floor, 1 Market Avenue, Chichester PO19 1JU

Telephone: 0845 1002617
Facsimile: 01243 779389

6

GROUNDS FOR SEEKING DISPENSATION

You will be given an opportunity later to give further details of your case and to supply the Tribunal with any documents that support it. At this stage you should give a clear outline of your case so that the Tribunal understands what your application is about. Please continue on a separate sheet if necessary.

1. Describe the qualifying works or qualifying long term agreement concerned stating when the works were carried out or are planned to be carried out or in the case of a long term agreement, the date that agreement was entered into or the proposed date it is to be entered into.

_____

_____

_____

_____

_____

_____

_____

_____

2. Describe the consultation that has been carried out or is proposed to be carried out.

_____

_____

_____

_____

_____

_____

_____

3. Explain why you seek dispensation of all or any of the consultation requirements

_____

_____

_____

_____

_____

_____

_____

_____

**Residential
Property**
TRIBUNAL SERVICE

**Application Form
Part IV Landlord and Tenant Act 1987
Application for the variation of a lease or leases**

This is the correct form to use if you want to ask the Leasehold Valuation Tribunal to vary a lease or leases under Part IV of the Landlord and Tenant Act 1987.

Please do not send any documents with this application form except for those specified in paragraph 6. If and when further evidence is needed you will be asked to send it in separately. If you have any questions about how to fill in this form or the procedures the Tribunal will use, please call us on 0845 600 3178. **Please send this completed application form together with the application fee and a copy of the documents to the appropriate panel (see page 6 for panel addresses).**

1. DETAILS OF APPLICANT(S) (if there are multiple Applicants please continue on a separate sheet)

Name _____

Address (including postcode) _____

_____

_____

Address for correspondence *(if different)* _____

_____

Telephone: *Day:* _____ *Evening:* _____ *Mobile:* _____

Email address: _____ Fax: _____

Capacity (e.g. landlord/tenant/management company) _____

Representative details _____

_____

_____

Where details of a representative have been given, all correspondence and communications will be with them until the tribunal is notified that they are no longer acting.

2. ADDRESS (including postcode) OF PROPERTY (if not already given)

_____

_____

_____

3. BRIEF DESCRIPTION OF PROPERTY *(e.g., 2-bedroom flat in Victorian block)*

_____

_____

_____

_____

1

4. DETAILS OF RESPONDENT(S) (all other current parties to the lease must be made defendants if there are multiple Respondents please continue below and on a separate sheet if required)

Name _____

Address (including postcode) _____

_____

_____

Address for correspondence *(if different)* _____

_____

_____

Telephone: *Day:* _____ *Evening:* _____ *Mobile:* _____

Email address *(if known)*: _____

Capacity *(e.g. landlord/tenant/managing agent)* _____

DETAILS OF RESPONDENTS (continued)

Name _____

Address (including postcode) _____

_____

_____

Address for correspondence *(if different)* _____

_____

_____

Telephone: *Day:* _____ *Evening:* _____ *Mobile:* _____

Email address *(if known)*: _____

Capacity *(e.g. landlord/tenant/management company)* _____

Name _____

Address (including postcode) _____

_____

_____

Address for correspondence *(if different)* _____

_____

_____

Telephone: *Day:* _____ *Evening:* _____ *Mobile:* _____

Email address *(if known)*: _____

Capacity *(e.g. landlord/tenant/management company)* _____

2

5. LEASE VARIATION(S) TO BE CONSIDERED BY THE TRIBUNAL

This form may be used for applications under section 35, 36, 37 and 40 of the Landlord and Tenant Act 1987

Please provide the following information on the attached sheet entitled "Lease Variation Details" or provide the details in a separate document.

(a) **the date of the lease, the relevant terms of the lease and a draft of the variation sought;**

(b) **the grounds of the claim;**

Please enclose the following documents with the application form:

(a) **Copies of the relevant lease(s);**

(b) **A list of the name and address of every person likely to be affected by the claim and a statement that each of those persons has been served with notice of the application.**

Guidance note:
Section 35 of the Landlord and Tenant Act 1985 and the LVT regulations require applicants to notify all persons known to him/her who are likely to be affected by the application that it is being made. Persons who are likely to be affected may include (but are not limited to) other lessees in the same block of flats or any mortgagee or superior landlord.

6. OTHER APPLICATIONS

Do you know of any other cases involving either: (a) the same or similar issues about the variation of a lease or leases as in this application; or (b) the same landlord or tenant or property as in this application? If so please give details.

7. LIMITATION OF COSTS

If you are a tenant, do you wish to make a s20C application *(see Guidance Notes)*   YES ☐   NO ☐

If so, why? _____

Guidance Notes
Some leases allow a landlord to recover costs incurred in connection with the proceedings before the LVT as part of the service charge. Section 20C of the Landlord and Tenant Act 1985 gives the tribunal power, on application by a tenant, to make an order preventing a landlord from taking this step. If you are a tenant you should indicate here whether you want the tribunal to consider making such an order.

3

8. CAN WE DEAL WITH YOUR APPLICATION WITHOUT A HEARING?

If the Tribunal thinks it is appropriate, and all the parties agree, it is possible for your application to be dealt with entirely on the basis of written representations and documents and without the need for parties to attend and make oral representations. This means you would not be liable for a hearing fee of £150 but it would also mean that you would not be able to explain your case in person. Please let us know if you would be happy for your application to be dealt with in this way.

I would be happy for the case to be dealt with
on paper if the Tribunal thinks it is appropriate   YES ☐   NO ☐

NB: Even if you have asked for a determination on paper the Tribunal may decide that a hearing is necessary. Please go on to answer questions 11 to 13 on the assumption that a hearing will be heard.

9. TRACK PREFERENCES

We need to decide whether to deal with the case on the Fast Track or the Standard Track.

(see Guidance Notes for an explanation of what a track is). Please let us know which track you think appropriate for this case.

Fast Track ☐   Standard Track ☐

Is there any special reason for urgency in this case? YES ☐   NO ☐

If there is, please explain how urgent it is and why: _____

_____

The Tribunal will normally deal with a case in one of three ways: on paper, on the "fast track", and on the "standard track." The fast track is designed for cases that need a hearing but are very simple and will not generate a great deal of paperwork or argument. A fast track case will usually be heard within 10 weeks of your application. You should indicate here if you think the case is very simple and can easily be dealt with. The standard track is designed for more complicated cases where there may be numerous issues to be decided or where, for example, a lot of documentation is involved. A standard track case may involve the parties being invited to a Pre-Trial Review which is a meeting at which the steps that need to be taken to bring the case to a final hearing can be discussed.

10. AVAILABILITY

If there are dates or days we must avoid during the next three months (either for your convenience or the convenience of any expert you may wish to call) please list them here.

Dates on which you will NOT be available _____

_____

_____

11. VENUE REQUIREMENTS

Please provide details of any special requirements you or anyone who will be coming with you may have (e.g., the use of a wheelchair and/or the presence of a translator) _____

_____

In London cases are usually heard in Alfred Place, which is fully wheelchair accessible. Elsewhere hearings are held in local venues which are not all so accessible and the Clerks will find it useful to know if you or anyone you want to come to the hearing with you has any special requirements of this kind.

12. CHECK LIST

Please check that you have completed this form fully. The tribunal will not process your application until this has been done. Please ensure that the following are enclosed with your application:

A copy of the lease(s) is/are enclosed ☐

A list of the names and address of persons affected and served with notice of this application is enclosed ☐

A draft of the variation(s) sought is enclosed ☐

Amount of fee enclosed _____ Please put your name and address on the back of any cheque you send.

DO NOT send cash under any circumstances. Cash payment will not be accepted and any application accompanied by cash will be returned to the applicant.

Please ONLY send this application form, a copy of the lease and the application fee and nothing else.

Guidance notes:
The amount of the application fee will depend on the number of dwellings to which the application relates. To find out how much you will need to pay you should consult the following table:

Number of dwellings to which application relates	Application Fee
5 or fewer dwellings	£150
Between 6 and 10 dwellings	£250
More than 10 dwellings	£350

Fees should be paid by a crossed cheque made payable to or a postal order drawn in favour of the Office of the Deputy Prime Minister.

Waiver and Fees
*You will **not** be liable to pay a fee if you or your partner is in receipt of:*
* *Income Support*
* *Housing Benefit*
* *Income Based Job Seeker's Allowance*
* *A working tax credit, and either:*
  * *you or your partner receive a tax credit with a disability or severe disability element; or*
  * *you or your partner is also in receipt of a child tax credit*
* *a guarantee credit under the State Pensions Credit Act 2002*
* *certificate issued under the Funding Code which has not been revoked or discharged and which is in respect of the proceedings before the tribunal the whole or part of which have been transferred from the county court for determination by a tribunal*
* *A Working Tax Credit where the Gross Annual Income used to calculate the Tax Credit is £14,213 or less*

If you wish to claim a waiver of fees you must complete another form available from the Panel office. The waiver form will not be copied to other parties in the proceedings.

If you are making several applications at the same time, even if you are using different application forms or the applications relate to different parts of the Tribunal's jurisdiction, you do not have to pay a separate fee for each application. The overall fee will be the biggest of the fees payable for each application on its own.

If you are in any doubt about the amount of fee or have any other questions about how to fill in this form please telephone the RPTS help line on 0845 600 3178.

13. STATEMENT OF TRUTH

I believe that the facts stated in this application are true.

Signed: _____ Dated: _____

5

PANEL ADDRESSES

Northern Rent Assessment Panel
20th Floor, Sunley Tower, Piccadilly Plaza, Manchester M1 4BE

Telephone: 0845 1002614
Facsimile: 0161 2367 3656

Midland Rent Assessment Panel
2nd Floor, East Wing, Ladywood House
45-46 Stephenson Street
Birmingham B2 4DH

Telephone: 0845 1002615
Facsimile: 0121 643 7605

Eastern Rent Assessment Panel
Great Eastern House, Tenison Road, Cambridge CB1 2TR

Telephone: 0845 1002616
Facsimile: 01223 505116

London Rent Assessment Panel
2nd Floor, 10 Alfred Place, London WC1E 7LR

Telephone 020 7446 7700
Facsimile 020 7637 1250

Southern Rent Assessment Panel
1st Floor, 1 Market Avenue, Chichester PO19 1JU

Telephone: 0845 1002617
Facsimile: 01243 779389

LEASE VARIATION DETAILS

PLEASE USE THE SPACE BELOW TO PROVIDE INFORMATION MENTIONED IN PART X OF THE MAIN APPLICATION FORM.

You will be given an opportunity later to give further details of your case and to supply the Tribunal with any documents that support it. At this stage you should give a clear outline of your case so that the Tribunal understands what your application is about. Please continue on a separate sheet if necessary.

The application is made under the Landlord and Tenant Act 1987;

Section 35 ☐
Section 36 ☐
Section 37 ☐
Section 40 ☐

The grounds of the claim _____

_____

_____

_____

_____

_____

The date and term of the lease(s) _____

_____

The relevant terms of the lease(s) _____

_____

_____

_____

_____

A draft of the variation(s) sought _____

_____

_____

_____

_____

**Residential
Property**
TRIBUNAL SERVICE

Ref no. (for office use only)

Application to the Leasehold Valuation Tribunal – (LVT)
Application for reduction or waiver of fees
(Paragraph 9(4) Schedule 12 Commonhold and Leasehold Reform Act 2002)

1. DETAILS OF PROPERTY/APPLICANT

Address of property (including postcode) _____

_____

Applicant name _____

Applicant address (including postcode) _____

_____

Date of application to LVT _____

(A)

Do you, or your partner [1], have a valid certificate under the
Funding Code issued in respect of the relevant proceedings which
have been transferred from the County Court? If so, please send a
copy to the LVT. You do not need to fill in the rest of this form.   YES ☐   NO ☐

Or

(B)

Are you, or your partner [1], in receipt of any of the following benefits?

	YOU	YOUR PARTNER
Income Support	☐	☐
Housing Benefit	☐	☐
Income-based Jobseeker's Allowance	☐	☐
Tax credit which is combined with:	☐	☐
A disability or a severe disability element (or both)	☐	☐
Child Tax Credit	☐	☐
Tax Credit where the Gross Annual Income used to calculate the Tax Credit is £14,213 or less	☐	☐
Guarantee Credit under the State Pensions Credit Act 2002	☐	☐

Please sign and date the agreement overleaf to allow the Benefits Agency or Local Authority to release the necessary
details to the Leasehold Valuation Tribunal for the purpose of verifying your claim to exemption from fees. Please
then take or send this form to the Leasehold Valuation Tribunal.

Note 1:
*'Partner' means the applicant's spouse or a person of the opposite sex with whom he or she lives as husband or wife or a person of the same
sex with whom he or she lives in a relationship which has the characteristics of the relationship between husband and wife.*

1

AGREEMENT TO PROVIDE THE LEASEHOLD VALUATION TRIBUNAL WITH DETAILS OF BENEFIT CLAIMS (Benefit claimant to complete).

I agree that the Benefits Agency/Local Authority may confirm to the _____ * Leasehold Valuation Tribunal that I was in receipt of the following benefit on the date of an application to the LVT by me or my partner, for the purpose of verifying a claim to a waiver of fees payable for an application.   *insert regional LVT*

Type of benefit received _____

Address of Office where I claim benefit _____

_____

_____

_____

My name (in capitals) _____

My address (in capitals) _____

_____

_____

_____

National Insurance Number _____

or Local Authority reference number (for Housing Benefit) _____

FOR BENEFIT AGENCY/LOCAL AUTHORITY COMPLETION

I certify that the above named benefit customer was in receipt of _____ (specify benefit) on _____ (date of application to LVT)

If benefit has ceased please give last date of entitlement _____

Signed _____

Section _____ Telephone number _____

Office Stamp

Form to be returned after completion in the envelope provided to:
_____ (LVT)

Address of Office where I claim benefit _____

_____

_____

_____

Telephone number _____

2

RPTS guidance on tenants' associations

TENANTS' ASSOCIATIONS

What is a Tenants 'Association?

A Tenants' Association is a group of tenants (lessees) who hold houses or flats on tenancies/leases from the same landlord upon similar terms which contain provisions for the payment of variable service charges. To be wholly effective an Association needs to be formally recognised.

What is the role of a recognised Association?

The members will have come to ether to represent their common interest so that the Association can with their consent and on their behalf:

- ask for a summary of costs incurred by their landlord in connection with matters for which they are being required to pay a service charge
- inspect the relevant accounts and receipts
- be sent a copy of estimates obtained by the landlord for intended work to their properties
- propose names of contractors for inclusion in any tender list when the landlord wishes to carry out major works
- ask for a written summary of the insurance cover and inspect the policy
- be consulted about the appointment or re-appointment of the agent managing the services.

How does an Association become recognised?

There are two ways of seeking recognition. The first of these is for an Association to ask the landlord for written notice of recognition. If this is given, then no further steps to establish recognition need be taken. Such recognition cannot be withdrawn by the landlord without first giving at least six months' notice to the Association. If however the landlord refuses or withdraws recognition, then the Association can apply for recognition to one of the five Rent Assessment Panels which constitute the Residential Property Tribunal Service (RPTS) and in whose region the properties are located. A list of the panels and their addresses is given in Annex 1.

How is application for recognition made to a panel?

An application form can be obtained from a panel office. The Association will need to supply with its application

(a) A copy of the Association's Constitution (Rules)

(b) A list of subscribing members 'names and their addresses
(c) The name and address of the landlord
(d) A description of the properties whose tenants will be eligible for membership (ie flats/houses) and their addresses
(e) Copies of any relevant previous correspondence with the landlord regarding recognition of the Association.

It should be noted that it is the panels 'practice to pass copies of documentation received from a party to any other interested party. It follows that correspondence written 'without prejudice' or 'in confidence' cannot be accepted.

Who will deal with the matter?

In the first instance, the application will be dealt with by the Clerks who comprise the administrative staff of the panel. They will deal with all correspondence and will continue to deal with the paperwork until the final decision is
reached. Clerks are able to speak to you about the processes and procedures
relating to the application. They cannot however give legal advice or advise
you about the law relating to your application.

Consideration of the application and the decision as to whether recognition
should be granted will be made by a member of the panel nominated by the
panel President or by the President personally. He or she will be a qualified
lawyer or valuer (a surveyor with experience of the management of housing
property).

Will recognition be given automatically?

No. The panel has a discretion as to whether recognition should be granted
and will need to be satisfied that the Rules of the Association are fair and
democratic –also that the actual membership of the Association will represent
a significant proportion of the potential membership. As a general rule, the
panel would expect the membership to be not less than 60% of those qualifying to join the Association.

What is meant by fair and democratic?

The panel will need to be satisfied that the Rules cover the following matters,
among others:
• Openness of membership
• Election of a Secretary, Chairman and any other Officers
• Payment and the amount of the subscription
• Obligatory Annual Meetings
• Notices of Meetings
• Voting arrangements and quorum. Only one vote per flat or house will be
permitted
• Independence from the landlord.

What form should the Association's rules take?

Annex 2 to this leaflet contains a set of model rules which you may find helpful in drawing up your own Constitution. They may need modification to suit
the particular circumstances of your Association and there is no obligation to

adopt them. You may prefer to draft your own Rules, but you must ensure that they meet the essential criteria set out in the previous paragraph.

Who will be eligible for membership of the Association?

There is no precise definition of tenants 'qualifications and each case must be considered on its merits. Basically a member must be contributing to the payment of a service char e levied by a landlord and which the landlord can, under the terms of similar leases/tenancies, vary from time to time to meet expenditure incurred or to be incurred in the maintenance, repair or insurance of a block or estate of dwellings in the landlord 's ownership. Tenants paying fixed rents which incorporate a non-variable service charge will not qualify for membership. Membership will not be open to landlords personally nor to persons connected with them (eg. employees of the landlord).

Tenants of shops or similar business premises (unless their tenancies incorporate residential accommodation)would not usually qualify. Membership of an Association may be extended to other individuals with a common interest (for example sub tenants)but they will not have voting rights and cannot be party to the proceedings of the Association in its role as a Recognised Association.

How is recognition by a panel given and for how long will it last?

The panel member appointed to consider the application will consider all the documentation submitted including any submission made by the landlord.

If that member is satisfied that recognition should be granted, he or she will issue a Certificate of Recognition. The length of validity of the Certificate is at the panel 's discretion but will usually be for four years. When the Certificate expires, the Association can apply for renewal. It is open to the panel to cancel a Certificate at any time if it is considered that for some reason the Association no longer merits recognition.

Can an estate have more than one recognised association?

In certain circumstances, more than one Association will be recognised where there is no duplication and the interests of tenants can be seen to differ – for example separate blocks of flats (but not separate Associations representing tenants in the same block).

Why form a tenants' association?

A landlord can be required to consult a recognised Association regarding such matters as service charges and management which would not be so in the case of individual tenants. It should also be helpful to a landlord to consult with an Association rather than to have to o to the greater trouble and expense of dealing with individual tenants.

What if there is a change of landlord?

The Association with a current Certificate of Recognition should serve a Notice on the new landlord if it still wishes to be consulted indicating the existence of a Certificate.

If the association is unhappy with the administration of its application to the panel, to whom should it complain?

If you have a complaint about the work of the panel you should write to the panel's President. You will receive an acknowledgement within two days of receipt of your complaint. A further appeal may be made from the decision of a President to a panel constituted from the RPTS Management Board. Such appeals should be addressed to:

The Senior President
RPTS
3rd Floor
Whittington House
19–30 Alfred Place
London WC1E 7LR

A full reply will follow within fifteen working days or you will be advised of the delay. If you remain dissatisfied, you are entitled to ask your MP to ask the Parliamentary Ombudsman to investigate your complaint.

What will it cost to make the application?

No charge is made by the panel but each party must meet their own costs.

Annex 1
PANELS AND THEIR ADDRESSES

Northern Rent Assessment Panel

President: Martin Davey LLB
Panel Secretary: Marj Foster and Alison Lomax (job share)
20th Floor, Sunley Tower, Piccadilly Plaza,
Manchester M1 4BE,

Telephone: 0845 1002614
Facsimile: 0161 237 3656

Midland Rent Assessment Panel

President: John Bettinson LLB
Panel Secretary: Maureen McCabe
2nd Floor, East Wing, Ladywood House,
45–46 Stephenson Street,
Birmingham B2 4DH

Telephone: 0845 1002615
Facsimile: 0121 643 7605

Eastern Rent Assessment Panel

President: Bruce Edgington
Panel Secretary: Ann Oates
Great Eastern House, Tenison Road,
Cambridge CB1 2TR

Telephone: 0845 1002616
Facsimile: 01223 505116

London Rent Assessment Panel

President: Siobhan McGrath
Panel Secretary: Donald Brown
Whittington House, 19–30 Alfred Place,
London WC1E 7LR

Telephone: 020 7446 7700
Facsimile: 020 7637 1250

Southern Rent Assessment Panel

President: Robert Long
Panel Secretary: Mark Sumner
1st Floor,1 Market Avenue,
Chichester PO19 1JU

Telephone: 0845 1002617
Facsimile: 01243 779389

Annex 2

SAMPLE DRAFT CONSTITUTION FOR AN ASSOCIATION OF TENANTS SEEKING RECOGNITION UNDER SECTION 29 OF THE LANDLORD AND TENANT ACT 1985

1 Name

The name of the Association shall be the 'The _____Residents' Association' ('the Association').

2 The property

All of the (houses and) flats, amenity areas and common areas of and at the premises known as

3 Objects of the Association

3.1 To promote and protect the common rights and interests of the members of the Association relating to the use and enjoyment of the Property.

3.2 To exercise the rights conferred upon the Association by recognition under the Landlord and Tenant Act 1985 or such other statutory rights that may be given by any subsequent enactment.

4 Membership

4.1 Membership shall be open to all persons who are lessees holding under long leases of a (house or) flat in the Property but voting shall be restricted to one vote for each (house or) flat.

4.2 Membership of the Association shall terminate:

4.2.1 upon a member giving written notice to that effect to the Honorary Secretary.

4.2.2 upon a member ceasing to be a lessee of a (house or) flat at the Property.

4.2.3 upon failure by a member to pay the annual subscription in respect of that (house or) flat for three months after the same shall become due and payable.

4.3 Membership of the Association shall be confirmed upon the payment of the first subscription and formal acceptance by the proposed member of the rules and constitution of the Association.

4.4 A copy of this constitution shall be given to each member.

4.5 The Committee may at its discretion extend associate membership to any other person or persons resident on the Property but such associate members shall not be elected as Officers or members of the Committee of the Association and shall not be entitled to any vote.

4.6 Neither the Landlord, the Landlord's representative, any company controlled by the Landlord nor any employee of the Landlord shall be a member or associate of the Association.

5 The Officers

5.1 The Officers of the Association shall comprise a Chairman, Honorary Secretary and Honorary Treasurer who shall be members of the Association.

5.2 The Officers shall be elected annually at the Annual General Meeting and shall serve for one year but may be re-elected.

6 The Committee

6.1 The Committee of the Association shall consist of not less than (three) nor more than (five) members of the Association and the Officers of the Association.

6.2 The Committee members shall serve for three years and shall retire in rotation. Retiring Committee members may be re-elected without re-nomination.

6.3 The Committee shall be empowered to co-opt on a temporary basis other members of the Association to form sub-committees to consider such matters as the Committee or the Association shall determine and the decisions of such sub-committees shall be ratified by the Committee before implementation.

6.4 A quorum for any meeting of the Committee shall be at least ( ) of whom at least two must be Officers.

6.5 The Committee shall implement the objects of the Association and the resolutions of the Association.

7 Elections

7.1 The election of the Officers and Committee shall take place at the Annual General Meeting.

7.2 Nominations for the appointment of Officers and for membership of the Committee shall be proposed and seconded by two members of the Association in writing and lodged with the Honorary Secretary fourteen days prior to the Annual General Meeting and shall include the written consent of the nominee.

7.3 The Committee shall be empowered to fill any casual vacancy occurring on the Committee or among the Officers and any person so appointed shall serve until the next Annual General Meeting of the Association.

8 Finances

8.1 The financial year of the Association shall end on _____ in each year.

8.2 Accounts shall be prepared for the Association each year and these shall be audited in accordance with proper audit practice.

8.3 Auditors shall be appointed at the Annual General Meeting. Officers and Committee members shall not be eligible for appointment as auditors.

8.4 The Accounts shall be ratified by the Association at the Annual General Meeting.

8.5 The property and funds of the Association shall be held and administered by the Committee.

8.6 A resolution of the Committee shall be sufficient authority for payments or the incurring of liability for payments up to a limit not exceeding ( ) hundred pounds. Beyond such limit the Committee shall seek approval of such expenditure by the Association either at the Annual General Meeting or at an Extraordinary General Meeting.

8.7 A banking account shall be opened in the name of the Association and all cheques shall be signed by an Officer and countersigned by a member of the Committee.

8.8 The annual subscription of the Association shall be decided for the ensuing year at the Annual General Meeting but shall not be altered save by a two-thirds majority of the members attending such a meeting.

9 Meetings

9.1 The Annual General Meeting of the Association shall be held not later than three months from the end of the financial year.

9.2 An Extraordinary General Meeting of the Association shall be convened at any time by the Honorary Secretary either upon the written instructions of the Committee or upon a written request signed by no fewer than (ten) members of the Association.

9.3 A quorum at an Annual General Meeting or an Extraordinary General Meeting shall be not less than twenty-five per cent of the membership – such quorum to be determined at the commencement of the meeting. This provision shall not be capable of amendment.

9.4 Fourteen days written notice of any General Meeting shall be delivered to each member of the Association to ether with an agenda.

9.5 The agenda shall comprise any draft resolution which it is proposed to be considered and (in the case of the Annual General Meeting) nominations for the Officers and Committee and a copy of the audited accounts for approval.

9.6 A record containing all resolutions and nominations to be moved at any General Meeting to ether with the names of those proposing and seconding each resolution or nomination shall be maintained by the Honorary Secretary; which record shall be made available for inspection by any member of the Association for seven days prior to the Annual General Meeting.

9.7 Minutes of all appointments of Officers and resolutions carried at Annual or Extraordinary General Meetings shall be taken. The Minute Book shall be open to inspection by any member of the Association who shall be entitled to take copies thereof.

9.8 Voting at meetings of the Association shall be by simple majority and by a show of hands unless a ballot is demanded by a majority. In the case of an equality of votes the Chairman shall have the casting vote.

10 Alterations to the rules and constitution

No alterations to the rules and constitution of the Association shall be made except at the Annual General Meeting or at an Extraordinary General Meeting and in any event no alteration to rules 8.8 and 9.3 of the constitution of the Association may be made.

11 Winding up

In the event of the Association being wound up any surplus funds shall be disbursed to a suitable registered charity to be decided by a simple majority of the membership.

Index